The learned arts of

WITCHES
& WIZARDS

The learned arts of

WITCHES
&
WIZARDS

History and traditions
of white magic

Anton & Mina Adams

MetroBooks

Contents

INTRODUCTION

Invisible forces shape our world, whether it be the change in the seasons, the moon's effect on the earth's seas or a particular chemistry between people in love.

To work magic is to understand these forces or energies, from the rage of a summer storm to the sexual tension felt between two people. Witches and wizards know how to use these energies and understand that magic is a very powerful tool – a big bite of the apple from the biblical Tree of Wisdom. Is it sinful or is it essential for the health of ourselves and the earth?

The terms "witch" or "wizard" have traditionally meant, respectively, a female or male worker of magic. In this book, we have linked the traditional term of witch to magic derived from the earth, such as the use of herbs and the practice of divination using natural objects. We have linked the traditional term of wizard to the magic of the scholar, of literate intellectuals of whom modern scientists are direct descendants. It is a world where the arts of mathematics, astrology, alchemy and ritual magic are all intertwined.

Historically, a wizard's aims might be to converse with angels or the ghosts of long-dead philosophers, to conjure spirits, to discern the fate of nations or to transmute base metal to gold. A witch's aims deal with conjuring a plentiful harvest, bringing fruitfulness to the village, brewing love potions and being an intermediary between the will of nature and that of the villagers.

In modern times, the term "witch" covers both sexes, and what witches believe is extremely varied. Witchcraft has now been reborn as "Wicca" – a term derived from an Old English word simply meaning "worker of sorcery". Each witch freely develops his or her own belief system. With the increase of information about the spirituality of other nations and times, the magic of traditional and ancient societies are culled for specific techniques, spells and invocations that appeal to a particular witch.

However, there are some areas of common ground, including the search for balance. Balance in terms of witchcraft is concerned with the balance between light and dark, the balance of the elements, such as earth, air, fire and water, and the balance between male and female energies. In Wicca, the forces of nature are personified by the figures of two deities, a goddess of the Earth and Moon and her consort, a horned god whose horns or antlers were symbolic of his affinity with the beasts of the forests, rather than indicative of diabolism. They are known by many names.

As a witch, wizard or novice, to understand the invisible forces, you must learn to think in a way different from that needed to survive in the everyday physical world. You must use your intuition and, most importantly, you must believe in your intuitive ability. Without this belief, magic will not happen.

It is also important to question your intention before casting a spell. This relates to whether you are going to practice white or black magic. White magic refers to the use of energies for constructive purposes, such as healing and helping people understand themselves. It is a satisfying magic to practice. Black magic is about the use of energies to impede or bind people or their actions. Modern witches and wizards are not inclined to attempt any form of destructive magic, believing that any spell sent out returns with thrice the potency upon the sender.

This book will help you develop the skills required to start your own journey into this fascinating world — a world that helps balance the body with the soul, a balance echoed in nature.

WITCHCRAFT – ITS PASSAGE THROUGH TIME

SORCERY IN ANCIENT TIMES

Roman Sorcerer or Talented Individual?

Sorcery is a word often used for practices of black magic designed to manipulate the cosmos for the sorcerer's own ends. The alleged exploits of such sorcerers stretch far back to the ancient worlds of Italy and Greece. Romanticized versions of their activities embody the desires of many people – the freedom to escape the drudgery of ordinary life and the power to make the extraordinary and the spectacular happen.

Not all sorcerers had evil intent. One notable benevolent sorcerer was the Roman poet, Publius Vergilius Maro (70–19 B.C.), otherwise known as Vergil. He was said to have learnt magic from 12 devils whom he released from a bottle found buried in his vineyard. He reputedly furthered his knowledge of magic by visiting a famous sorcerer who lived on the Mountain of Sorrows; he later founded a school for sorcerers in Naples.

Vergil's reputed exploits involving magic are very colorful and worthy of Hollywood. In these adventures, he was allegedly a hard man to trap, transfixing pursuers on the spot, disappearing into a pail of water and escaping from prison by sailing away in a boat drawn on the wall of his cell. He was famous for making various magical talismans, such as a golden leech that successfully protected the city of Naples from a leech plague. His powers also included making inanimate objects animate, such as iron or copper horses that could cure diseases or trample thieves, and metal statues that were said to have guarded his treasure.

To what extent his exploits contained the elements of truth will never be known. Was he merely a gifted metalsmith ahead of his time, good at sleight of hand, or did he indeed find a bottle of helpful demons in the backyard?

The ancient practice of magic existed before the Greek and Roman empires and predates Christianity. However, pragmatic Christian theologians, such as St. Augustine, were often depicted artistically in a magical light to give them greater mythical proportions.

Mythical Greek Sorceresses –
Tales of Treachery, Beauty and Vengeance

Tales of sorcery also appeared in the myths of ancient Greece. Two of the most powerful sorceresses of Greek mythology are Circe and her niece Medea. Both are the daughters or priestesses of Hecate, a goddess of the waning and dark moon who came to be the patroness of witchcraft.

Living on an island as an exile, Circe learned the art of magic. Her magic centered around the use of her female charms, such as her beautiful hair, which helped her control the creative and destructive forces. Circe is linked in mythology to the exploits of Odysseus who, on his travels home after the Trojan wars, arrived on Circe's island. His men were turned into swine, the result of a spell cast by Circe. However, Odysseus was saved from the same fate because of his having eaten a magical herb. With some forceful coercion from Odysseus, Circe lifted her spell over his men, but she was successful in keeping Odysseus from his travels back to his wife for one year.

In art, Circe is depicted as a beautiful woman who carries a magician's wand and is surrounded by men turning into animals.

Circe offers a cup of poison to Odysseus with his companions. A woodcut from the Nuremberg Chronicle by Hartmann Schedel (1440 – 1514).

Medea, 1873, by Anselm Feuerbach (1829 – 80).

Medea

Medea was a vengeful sorceress who used magic potions and some trickery to achieve her own ends. One story in Greek mythology has her making her lover, Jason, invincible for one day by the use of a magical ointment so he could win the Golden Fleece.

She is often depicted in art as standing over a bubbling cauldron, making an old ram young. The myth has her cutting the ram into pieces while speaking magical incantations over them as they boiled into the shape of a lamb. The rejuvenation spell was actually a trick to lure her enemy, Pelias the King of Iolcus, into believing that the spell would also make him young again. It is not surprising that Medea disappeared before saying the appropriate spell, leaving behind her enemy's corpse.

CELTIC AND ANGLO-SAXON WITCHCRAFT

Guardian of the Land – the Mystery of Merlin

A popular myth in many cultures is that of a powerful guardian who helps guide the country's rulers. In Britain, that guardian takes the form of Merlin, one of the world's best known wizards. His exact origins are unknown and he has featured in literary works since the early twelfth century, particularly in the works of Geoffrey of Monmouth and later Sir Thomas Malory. Monmouth, who wrote the "Prophesies of Merlin" in the 1130s, refers to Merlin as a prophet living in the fifth or sixth century, who was credited with using magic to bring the stones from Ireland to build Stonehenge.

Through the ages, Merlin has become the archetypal wise old man who may appear in the guise of a man or an animal, such as a hawk, to help or advise modern witches and wizards working with Celtic magic. The Celtic pantheon, unlike the Greek, Roman or Egyptian gods and goddesses, prefer not to be invoked but to appear when and where they feel they are needed.

The Celtic pantheon included the other historical participants of the Arthurian saga, such as Arthur, Lancelot and the Knights of the Round Table, mainly in the form of a mythic archetype – for example, Arthur is seen as the hero sun warrior.

However, in its earliest form, the Celtic pantheon consisted of the goddess (Mother Earth) and the god. The goddess was revered in all of her three aspects – Maid (virgin), Mother (wife) and Crone (wise woman). The god was revered in both his roles as Lord of the Sun and Lord of the Underworld.

The Beguiling of Merlin from 'Idylls of the King' by Alfred Tennyson (1809 – 92),
c. 1870 – 74, by *Sir Edward Burne-Jones (1833 – 98)*.

The Reverence of Nature in Celtic Magic

The main element of Celtic magic is the reverence of nature. Each stream, stone, tree and flower is given a name and a personality, and each is held to be sacred. The movement of animals are studied for omens. Streams are believed to be sanctuaries of the Celtic fertility goddess. Natural objects and animals are accorded a wisdom and knowledge we now lack, and Celtic magic develops a language where people can again become attuned to the ebbs and flows of nature.

It is a fundamental belief that you must be linked with the land under your feet before you can work with Celtic magic. A good way to link in with the land is to learn tree magic. Meditating while sitting, leaning against the trunk of a tree, is a powerful way of linking into the earth. Imagine that the trunk of the tree and the trunk of your body are one and that the energy in your spine continues into the earth through the roots of the tree.

In Celtic magic, each tree has its own character and corresponding purpose. The willow, for example, was planted to guard the home against hostile elements. Animals are also important magical guides. There are a number of historical sites throughout the United Kingdom which are linked to a Celtic magical past, including various hill figures.

A frequent theme for hill figures is a white horse. The most famous of this figure is the White Horse of Uffington in Berkshire, England. It is thought that this horse was cut by the Celts in the first century B.C. The purpose behind its construction is still unclear, with many followers of Celtic lore maintaining that the White Horse of Uffington could be used astrologically or as the sacred site of tribal gatherings. There is also a legend that if you stand on the eye of the Horse and turn three times clockwise while keeping your eyes closed and making a wish, your wish will come true within a period of seven days, seven weeks, seven months or even seven years.

White Horse Hill, Uffington, 1992, by Evangeline Dickson (living artist).
The White Horse is cut into a chalk hill and measures 360 feet (approximately
110 meters) from the tip of its tail to its nose.

TRADITIONAL SOCIETIES

Well-Defined Roles in Village or Community Life

In non-Western societies, white witchcraft had its defined and necessary functions within village or community life. Specific roles were filled by people who had either shown ability or who were born to the role. In many traditional societies, the roles of shaman, shamanka (the female equivalent), witchdoctor, medicine man and wise woman were accepted and respected. Healing, midwifery, and the assurance of good crops were important functions required by the village.

However, a central role of the shaman or witchdoctor is the protection of the village from evil spirits and the evil of humankind. He or she would be called upon to diagnose whether a person or animal was being harmed by black magic. In many traditional societies, there is a belief that any illness or misfortune could be attributed to the actions of an evil sorcerer. To identify who was psychically attacking the victim, the shaman or witchdoctor would use one of a number of rituals in his or her repertoire, including invoking a trance state through dancing, drumming or using locally grown hallucinogenic substances. By being in a trance state, the shaman or witchdoctor achieves an out-of-body experience in which they can see the solution to the problem without the distractions of everyday life. He or she is then in a good position to banish evil charms and spells.

Voluntary spirit possession could also be used when the help of spirits, usually earth spirits or ghosts, is necessary. It was thought that a spirit would talk to the shaman or witchdoctor if he or she allowed his or her body to be possessed by the particular spirit in question. Sometimes blood sacrifices were necessary to aid in the possession of the spirit and to hear its wisdom. It was thought that a blood sacrifice released energy at the point of death that could be used for a specific magical purpose.

The Flyer *(an American Indian shaman)*, *c.1570, by* John White *(fl.c. 1570 – 93)*.

Native American Magic and the Shamanic Tradition

Literature concerning the shamanic tradition of the Native Americans has identified the emergence of a New Age self-help movement known as neoshamanism. Neoshamanism merges Wicca with shamanism, acknowledging their common strong focus on the worship and knowledge of nature. Shamanism has been described as a series of techniques rather than as a religion. The traditions of the Native Americans vary from tribe to tribe, with many tribes seeking to safeguard their rituals and the work of their shamans or shamankas from non-tribal members.

Nevertheless, anthropologists have noted that the beliefs of shamans are remarkably consistent from culture to culture. It is generally accepted that the shaman is chosen by the spirits. There are several ways in which this manifests, for example, after a person has experienced a serious life-threatening illness or a near-death experience. Sometimes the illness is preceded by a vision of the shaman's own death, when the soul begins its travels. The shaman then brings back a certain song or dance that is the essence of his or her power as a shaman. If the chosen person does not heed the call to become a shaman then his or her illness will become worse until he or she is facing death. If the challenge is accepted, the new shaman will find that his or her tools will appear. The shaman's tools of trade include a drum and rattle, fur and claws, and a "soul catcher". The soul catcher represents one of the functions of the shaman, that is, to retrieve lost souls.

The shaman's astral world consists of three levels which correlate to different types of spirit guides that he or she can contact for wisdom or solutions to problems belonging to members of his or her village. The "upper world" consists of teacher guides. The "middle world" is inhabited by the recently dead or concerned ancestors who are now stripped of earthly concerns but still linked with the earthly plane and willing to share their wisdom. The "lower world" consists of "power animals".

The eagle is a popular power animal for those seeking insight.

Power Animals

A power animal is an animal or thought form of an animal with specific psychic attributes or protective qualities, such as the eagle which symbolizes keen vision. The shaman is often associated with birds and some wear masks to connect with such power animals as the eagle, hawk, owl or raven.

The choice of power animal by a shaman relates to what aspects of an animal he or she wishes to utilize on his or her astral journey. The hawk is symbolic of clear vision and prophesy, the owl is also symbolic of prophesy and divination, while the raven is known for its ability to spot lost souls.

When the shaman's soul is released from the body, the soul loses the shape of the body and takes on that of an animal. Many shamans connect with their own power animal, finding that the animal helps them "ground", a term meaning to reconnect the body with the earth. There is a distinct danger in failing to ground properly, as it may result in physical damage to the body. To strengthen the connection with the power animal, a shaman conjures the animal who had already accepted the invitation to become his or her power animal, and performs a dance combined with monotonous trance-inducing drumming.

Many tribes are guarded by their own tribal power animal.

African and Caribbean Magic

In African magic, most tribes believe in a supreme being who created the world and who rules over lesser deities. Each deity or earth spirit is linked with a natural phenomenon or a particular animal. The devastation of volcanoes and the fear engendered by snakes have made these very powerful symbols.

Serpent worship was common in Africa, and when this type of magic came to certain islands of the Caribbean with the black slave trade, it evolved into the cult of voodoo. The word voodoo or *vodoun* is said to have been traced from a West African term meaning spirit or deity. The voodoo cult has a large pantheon of gods called *loas*. The most important *loas* are Danbhalah-Wedo, also known as the Great Serpent; Papa Legba, the god of the sun; and Baron Samedi, lord of the dead.

The loas are revered divinities who receive offerings.

The Loas The *loas* could be benevolent and wise, but there were some who were also violent and vindictive. A distinct group of the *loas* are the *guedes,* who are the spirits of death, debauchery and cemeteries. A strong image of the *guedes* is the figure of Baron Samedi, who is often depicted as a dapper undertaker dressed formally in a tailcoat and wearing a top hat.

Voodoo In Haiti, arguably the home of the purest form of voodoo practice, the voodoo rites are usually performed in special houses that feature a central post. To entice the spirits to descend to the earthly plane, special symbols called *ververs* are drawn on the floor, creating a doorway through which the spirits can pass. Prayers are sent to Papa Legba, who is also the guardian at the gate, much like Saint Peter with his keys to heaven, to allow the spirits to pass through the door.

When voodoo magic began to be feared by the white masters of the black slaves, many Africans were baptized into the Catholic faith. All this achieved was to increase the pantheon of powerful spiritual figures called upon in voodoo rites, such as Jesus, the Virgin Mary and many of the saints.

The practice of voodoo is essentially hereditary and is oriented toward the solving of everyday issues, such as finding or keeping a job or discovering the perfect partner. Sometimes, in an attempt to stop a person from hurting another, dolls are made in human form tied with cord or stuck with pins in strategic areas.

Zombies The creation of zombies is also part of voodoo belief. One tradition says that zombies are made when the person dies after having had his or her soul sucked out of his or her body. The creator of the zombie can reanimate the corpse by a certain procedure that does include a few knocks to the head. The creature is then forced to work tirelessly without any will power or pleasure, an interesting correlation with how the slaves would have felt when brought out to America and the Caribbean.

Spiritual Possession Many of the voodoo ceremonies are aimed at appeasing certain spirits and at accessing the knowledge of the loas by temporary spiritual possession. Spiritual possession is very different from demonic possession in a number of ways; for example, the spirit is consciously invited into the participant and the spirit's purpose is to educate, to give pronouncements on the future, or the solution to a particular question posed to it. In a case of demonic possession, the intent of the spirit is evil and invasive.

EARLY EUROPEAN AND AMERICAN WITCHCRAFT

With the rise of the Christian Church in England and Europe, the link between human beings and the earth began to disintegrate. By replacing the old pagan or Celtic earth religions with its more patriarchal system of worship, the Church taught that the streams, trees and stones had no inherent wisdom and that animals, believed by the Church to have no souls, were inferior creatures to human beings.

In an attempt to convert pagans to the Christian faith, the Church built on pagan sites and timed many of their major festivals with pagan celebrations — for instance, Christmas replaced the festival of Yule which is a pagan winter solstice celebration marking the birth of the sun god to the earth goddess.

In a subsequent attempt to consolidate power, the Church launched a strong attack against heretics. Groups and individuals who did not conform to the Church's teachings were punished as heretics and sentenced to death. Groups, such as the Cathars, who believed that the God of the Old Testament was the Devil and that the Catholic Church was worshiping him, were regarded as Satanists and virtually wiped out. Witches also came to be seen as Satanists throughout the thirteenth and fourteenth centuries. The distinction between white and black magic was disregarded, and natural magic, previously thought of as morally neutral, was, from the fifteenth century, considered demonic.

By 1484 a papal bull was issued by Pope Innocent VIII, identifying witches with heretics and the worship of the Devil. This edict and a publication called *Malleus Maleficarum* were to spearhead the Inquisition across Europe. Persecutions eventually came to an end in the 1730s — the Age of Reason.

Persecutions in England and Europe – "practyse of the blacke scyence"

The nature of witchcraft was the subject of the works of numerous theologians during the thirteenth and fourteenth centuries. The famous thirteenth-century theologian Thomas Aquinas believed that witches entered into pacts with the Devil, which enabled them to fly on broomsticks, raise storms and change into animals. Witches were likely to be blamed for any damage, illness or death suffered by the villagers or their animals, and even for natural disasters. In Europe, such accused witches were burned at the stake.

Persecutions against witchcraft in Europe were vicious and resulted in the deaths of tens of thousands of women, paupers and beggars. The *Malleus Maleficarum*, written by two German Inquisitors, provided rules for the identification, torture and murder of witches. Generally, witches and sorcerers were accused of numerous perverse practices, such as cannibalism and infanticide, as well as the renunciation of Christianity. In Europe, the prosecutions peaked between 1560 and 1660.

The persecution of witchcraft in England was not as malicious as in Europe and the hysteria against witches peaked during the 1640s. The second of three witchcraft Acts was passed in 1563, and it was soon after that a major witch trial was brought before the Chelmsford Assizes in 1566. Three women were charged with witchcraft, all on the testimony of a 12 year-old girl. Elizabeth Francis, Agnes Waterhouse and her daughter Joan were accused of consorting with a cat named Sathan which, apparently, could talk and cause the death and illness of various neighboring villagers. Only Agnes was hanged.

The publication of the Malleus Maleficarum *resulted in the death of many innocent people.*

Persecutions in America – the Salem "Witches"

It was not until the 1640s that the American colonies experienced any hysteria concerning witchcraft, possibly influenced by the English situation at the same time. The first witch was hanged in Connecticut in 1647 and there were scattered accounts of witches tried in other colonies. However, the most important witch trial was that of the Salem "witches" in Massachusetts from 1692 to 1693. Unrest in Massachusetts after the loss of its colonial charter in 1684, compounded by a number of social problems and repressions, led to a society ripe for accusations of witchcraft.

Over 200 people were arrested and accused of witchcraft. Nineteen were actually hanged, all on the testimony of a group of eight girls, ranging in age from 12 to 20, who claimed to see spectral emanations from those they accused of witchcraft. The girls, including Abigail Williams and Ann Putnam, were alleged to fall into frenzied convulsions if a "witch" came anywhere near them. Their convulsions would stop upon the touch of the witch's hand. Men and women died on this evidence alone. Wild stories abounded of normally law-abiding and churchgoing parishioners making pacts with the Devil. People were at first tried before Salem Town magistrates and then, once Massachusetts regained its charter, a Court was especially established to put the accused on trial.

As the number of accused witches grew, the juries and the public began to be doubtful about whether the girls' evidence was reliable. Questions were asked, particularly when the girls started accusing prominent people – such as Lady Phips, the wife of the royal governor – of witchcraft, and also when they accused those who had been publicly skeptical of the trials. Governor Phips dissolved the Court, and by 1703 the colony apologized and reparations were made to those accused of witchcraft and their families. It was interesting that many of the accusers suffered illnesses and much unhappiness after the end of the trials.

Illustration of the trial of two "witches" at *Salem* by *Howard Pyle*.
The Salem Trials became historically viewed as an abysmal travesty
of justice rather than an heroic fight against the Devil.

MEDIEVAL AND MODERN MAGICIANS

Magicians or Charlatans?

Magicians practice magic, a practice with as many variations as there are magicians. Fundamentally, magicians attempt to influence the future either by using spirits or natural forces. There was a profound link between the sciences, magicians and the Church during the medieval period. Priests were, however, forbidden to become magicians, astrologers and mathematicians from as early as 364 A.D.

With the advent of the printing press, the works of four important medieval magicians were published. These magicians — Agrippa von Nettesheim and Theophrastus Paracelsus in Europe; Dr. John Dee and Robert Fludd in England — enjoyed a certain notoriety but there were those, such as Faust and the Count of Saint-Germaine, who were considered charlatans.

Faust

According to one school of thought, Faust is a fictional character, an archetype of the powerful ancient magician, who made a pact with the Devil for greater knowledge and power. During the first half of the sixteenth century, there were many accounts of men who called themselves Faust, ranging from necromancers — those who summon the spirits of the dead — to drunken braggarts. Faust's fame was assured by a book of his exploits published in Frankfurt in 1587. It was curious that a number of Faust's powers and deeds in the book were the same as those attributed to such ancient sorcerers as Merlin and Vergil.

Count Saint-Germaine

Count Saint-Germaine's claim to fame was due more to his supposed immortality and his ability to survive without food — drinking only a secret elixir which gave him immortal life — than his skill as a magician. He made a deep impression as a brilliant conversationalist on the court of Louis XV in the eighteenth century, and the nobility were intrigued by his reputation of being much older than he looked. It is thought that his knowledge of and interest in history enabled him to tell anecdotes of historical events as if he were there, allowing him to imply that he was over 300 years old.

Agrippa (1486–1535) — Will Power and Imagination in Practicing Magic

Henry Cornelius Agrippa von Nettesheim was born in Cologne in 1486, the same year the *Malleus Maleficarum* was published. By the time he was 24 he had summed up all contemporary magical thinking in a manuscript entitled *De Occulta Philosophia* (On Occult Philosophy), which was published 20 years later. This manuscript was to have a profound effect on western occult thinking. Agrippa believed that magic had nothing to do with the Devil, but that the practice of magic relied on will power, imagination and the knowledge of nature's harmonies.

Agrippa was known to have practiced astrology, numerology and divination. His divinatory practices, particularly his fondness for necromancy, led to his reputation as a black magician. Necromancy encompasses the practice of contacting the dead or reanimating dead bodies. His activities were legendary and were at times linked with the Faust myth. One story concerns a young man who, while the magician was away, talked his way into Agrippa's study to read a book of spells. Inadvertently, by reading one spell aloud, the youth found himself staring at a very angry demon who demanded to know why he was summoned. The youth hesitated and was attacked by the demon who strangled him to death. Upon his return, Agrippa found the dead man in his study and summoned the demon to return life to the corpse for a period just long enough to enable it to walk out of the study and into the marketplace below. Unfortunately, the corpse collapsed. Despite his efforts, Agrippa was still suspected of murder and hounded out of town.

Paracelsus (1493–1541) – Healing Power of Natural Magic

Paracelsus, born Phillipus Aureolus Theophrastus Bombastus von Hohenheim, was a doctor, a natural healer who practiced in the early sixteenth century. He was not an active magician as such, but some of his theories about the connection of man with the universe were important concepts for future witches and wizards. As an alchemist, he believed that the soul, as well as the body, should be treated to cure an illness. In his youth he sought an elixir called Catholicon, a fabled potion that could heal any illness. During his search he developed potions to cure some of the common blights of Renaissance Europe by successfully incorporating minerals such as mercury. In 1536, despite accusations of charlatanism and exhibitionism, his work on his medical theories, *Die Grosse Wundartzney*, was finally published. His theories brought him some popularity.

Paracelsus held that health was achieved when there was harmony between humankind and nature. He was particularly interested in humanity's interrelationship with the cosmos, which he called the *Diva Matrix*, thus classifying it as the female element. Paracelsus studied astrology, believing that the stars and the planets profoundly influenced all life and matter. He was also fascinated by natural magic, describing it as a power coming directly from God, which could be channeled through a doctor to effect healing. Paracelsus emphasized the power of the imagination which could tap into the universe as reflected in humankind, and which could lead to self-discovery.

FAMOSO DOCTOR PARESELSVS

Portrait of the Physician Paracelsus by Quentin Massys (c.1466 – 1530).
Paracelsus' beliefs marked him as a man born ahead of his time.

Dr. John Dee (1527–1608) – Conversing With Angels

Dr. John Dee was known to be a scholar rather than a practitioner of magic. He lived in Elizabethan England, acting as an astrologer to Queen Elizabeth I. He was particularly influenced by the writings of Agrippa, but believed that he did not have the psychic powers to speak to spirits or angels. Dee instead used mediums of varying ability and degrees of honesty to help him contact the spirits. He was always financially unstable, and the bulk of his conversations with the spirits revolved around the finding of buried treasure or the Philosopher's Stone. The Philosopher's Stone is supposedly a substance that can turn anything into gold, cure all illnesses, and give immortal life.

One of Dee's most infamous mediums was an unsavoury character called Edward Kelly. Kelly claimed that he could summon spirits by scrying in a crystal or a special mirror. Dee recorded the various techniques used to speak with the spirits. During the sessions, the spirits, through Kelly, were able to spell out a message. Kelly advised dictating the message backward, claiming that uncontrollably dangerous forces would be unleashed if the message were directly dictated.

Eventually Kelly and Dee claimed that they discovered a secret language called Enochian, the letters of which corresponded with numerical values, the four elements of earth, air, fire and water, and the planets. The system of Enochian magic today involves practitioners seeking a higher plane of being by using the right Enochian incantation to the appropriate angel guarding that plane.

Robert Fludd (1574–1637) – Important English Hermeticist

Robert Fludd was an English astrologer living during the reign of Elizabeth I. He was greatly taken with the ideas of Hermes Trismegistus, the Greek equivalent of the Egyptian god Thoth. Trismegistus means "three times great". Legend has it that Hermes Trismegistus wrote the *Corpus Hermeticum,* a Greek manuscript that promoted humankind's power over nature through the use of astrological and alchemical principles. Until 1614, it was thought that these Hermetic theories were pre-Christian in origin.

Fludd believed that there was a strong link between the cosmos and humankind. He wrote *Ultiusque Cosmi Historia,* which included fascinating diagrams attempting to illustrate this interdependence, such as showing man linked to the sun with his heart and to the moon with his reproductive system, calling the cosmos Macrocosm and man Microscosm.

Aleister Crowley (1875–1947) – The Beast 666

Although famous for his later career, which was dogged by a heavy drug habit and insatiable sexual appetites, Aleister Crowley still made an important contribution to the practice of magic. His main problem was that he understood the power of magic but lacked the discipline to use the power without self-destructing.

He had a clever, inquiring mind, making a full-time study of the kabbala, Enochian magic, Hermetica, ceremonial magic and Egyptian occultism. He was also a prolific writer, *Book of the Law* being one of his most famous publications. Crowley claimed that the material was dictated to him by his Holy Guardian Angel. The book's central premise is that there is no law beyond "Do What Thou Wilt", which meant "follow your true will" not, as it is sometimes interpreted, "do whatever you want".

A very ambitious person, Crowley sought recognition for his self-perceived magical powers and was very competitive with his magical peers. He believed that he was a reincarnation of certain magicians, such as Eliphas Levi, a nineteenth-century French occultist who died on the same day as Crowley's birth.

Crowley was involved with many streams of magical philosophies of the early-twentieth century, and was initiated into the Second Order of the Hemetic Order of the Golden Dawn and the Ordo Templi Orientis (O.T.O.). He set up the English branch of the O.T.O. and rewrote many of the O.T.O.'s rituals, borrowing liberally from his *Book of the Law.*

Crowley is also thought to have made Gerald Gardner, the father of modern witchcraft, an honorary member of the O.T.O. It has been conjectured that Gardner and Crowley collaborated on the famous *Book of Shadows,* a book that Gardner had published as traditional material allegedly copied through the ages by witches. It has been pointed out the so-called traditional material was in fact borrowed from Crowley's *Book of the Law* and other writings by him. Another influential book by Crowley was *Magick in Theory and Practice.*

RENEWAL OF INTEREST IN THE NINETEENTH AND TWENTIETH CENTURIES

At the beginning of the nineteenth century, enormous changes in attitudes to magic were occurring. High magic — that is interest in magical systems such as astrology and numerology, was considered, at best, a prototype form of science. Low magic — earth- or nature-based magic — was seriously undermined by the Industrial Revolution. The magic which made perfect sense to a farmer in a field of grain made much less sense to a city-dwelling factory worker.

However, a reaction soon set in against the grimness of industrialization. A romanticized version of the forgotten wisdom of the ancient and medieval worlds led to the revival of a number of magical traditions. Paganism was a popular Romantic theme but it was high magic, in its new guise of ritual or ceremonial magic, that first showed signs of recovery. A great influx of Asian mystical and spiritual teachings flowed into the Western world throughout the nineteenth century. Secret societies and esoteric orders of all shapes and sizes became popular in Britain, Europe and America. In Germany and Great Britain there was a melding of European paganism and Jewish kabbalistic traditions. The kabbala is a Jewish traditional system that explains the creation of the world and the essence of the flow of energy through human beings and nature. It is a system that was adopted by many European occultists during the fifteenth and sixteenth centuries.

Folk magic was reborn as Wicca in the middle of the twentieth century, largely through the writings and rituals of an amateur folklorist named Gerald Brousseau Gardner. Gardner built on the ideas of Margaret A. Murray, who had some decades earlier written about the existence of an underground pagan faith of European folk magic, which she called the Dianic cult.

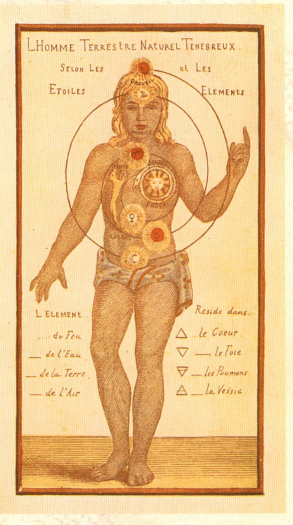

Illustration from Theosophica Practica, *19th century, showing the seven* Chakras. *A number of nineteenth-century societies and esoteric orders looked to the East for spiritual inspiration.*

Hermetic Order of the Golden Dawn

The Hermetic Order of the Golden Dawn was a small, short-lived organization that was particularly influential during the late-nineteenth and early-twentieth centuries. This secret Order collected an impressive repository of Western magical knowledge, encouraging potential initiates to make a serious study of magic. Numerous magical systems were taught. Many of these systems, such as Enochian magic (the language of angels), the Key of Solomon (conjuring spirits) and Abra-Melin magic (conjuring and taming demons) were allegedly based on parts of the kabbala.

The key purpose of the Order was to obtain the control of one's own nature and power. A hierarchy was established that followed the sephiroth of the Tree of Life of the kabbala. The Tree of Life is a multifaceted concept that explains the flow of energy between four worlds. Energy descends from the World of Origins (the world of the gods) through the World of Creation and the World of Formation to the World of Expression (our material world).

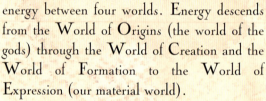

The origins of the Order are highly romantic, in part due to the discovery by one of its founders, Dr. William Wynn Westcott, of an "ancient manuscript" that contained partial rituals for the "Golden Dawn". The Golden Dawn captured the imagination of Westcott and a number of his friends, including Samuel MacGregor Mathers, and soon it was given a history and became known as an old German occult order. The Isis-Urania Temple of the Order was established in London, attracting members such as Aleister Crowley and the poet W.B. Yeats.

An outfit worn by some members of the Golden Dawn.

Theosophical Society

The Theosophical Society was founded in New York in 1875 by Russian spiritualist Madame Helena Blavatsky and others to promote a mix of Eastern and Western mysticism and spiritualism. The word "theosophy" had been used since ancient Greek times to refer to a special knowledge of the divine and was used by the Society to mean a secret knowledge that had been passed down through the ages. Within the Society a core group developed and they were able to study certain secret teachings. The Society was particularly interested in Eastern mysticism, especially from India and Tibet, and encouraged belief in such Eastern concepts as reincarnation. Madame Blavatsky claimed that her knowledge of the occult was given to her by dead ancestral masters called Mahatmas, during a journey through Tibet. She was also well read in occult literature.

The Society's membership flourished after the publication of Madame Blavatsky's first major work *Isis Unveiled.* Subtitled "A Master Key to the Mysteries of Ancient and Modern Science and Theology", the book promoted the study of Eastern religions. Despite the Eastern influence, the Society theoretically encouraged the study of a number of religions and philosophies and did not dictate any particular dogma. One of its aims is to "investigate the hidden mysteries of nature and the physical powers latent in mankind". The Society soon established Lodges in other countries and eventually moved its headquarters from New York to Adyar in India.

FAMOUS WITCHES OF THE TWENTIETH CENTURY

Gerald Brousseau Gardner (1884–1964) – the Father of Modern Witchcraft

Gerald Gardner is responsible for evolving a form of witchcraft called Wicca, which reflected his belief that witchcraft was the remains of an old ancient religion. While a member of an already existing coven in the New Forest area in England, Gardner put together a "Book of Shadows" explained various rituals and the raising of energy for the purposes of white magic. A Book of Shadows is a journal kept by a witch for the purposes of fine-tuning his or her practices. Although Gardner attempted to pass off the Book, published as *Lady Sheba's Book of Shadows,* as an ancient manuscript passed down from witch to witch, it was soon seen that he had merely pulled together material from such diverse sources as Celtic mythology and Aleister Crowley's works.

Gardner has been accused of being a charlatan, a voyeur and a masochist; however, many of his ideas have proven effective in the practice of white magic. Many modern-day witches borrow only certain aspects from his *Book of Shadows,* the most important being the equal worship of a god and a goddess whom he called Aradia and the working of magic in the nude.

Gardner advocated working "skyclad", a translation of an Indian term meaning "without clothes". It was explained that by working without clothes – clothes symbolizing the trappings of personality and everyday life – a witch was able to concentrate on his or her magical purpose.

Gardner also advocated the Great Rite in certain rituals. The Great Rite is the sexual union between two consenting adults during a ritual to raise a powerful energy which is then directed to the purpose of the ritual, such as a healing or the success of a spell. Originally, the Rite was performed before other participants and, of course, attracted enormous sensationalist publicity and claims of voyeurism. Many Wiccans now perform the Great Rite in private or symbolically, by dipping the athame, symbolizing male energy, into the chalice, female energy.

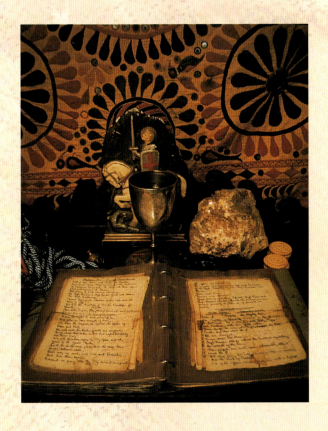

Gardner's Book of Shadows *provided the basis for many modern witchcraft traditions.*

Alex Sanders (1926–1988) – King of the Witches

Claiming to have been initiated as a witch at the age of seven by his grandmother, Alex Sanders created a sensationalist mythology around himself and his practices, which brought worldwide attention to Wicca. Taking up Gardner's ideas of witchcraft, Sanders created a theatrical version of Wicca that appealed to the British press in the 1960s, culminating in a claim that his initiates, allegedly numbering well over 1,500, wished him proclaimed as "King of the Witches". In Gardnerian covens, it was usual that a person desiring to be a witch had to undergo three levels of initiation that required study and training. During the 1960s, Sanders initiated many into Wicca without these requirements. However, modern-day Wiccans who wish to be known as Alexandrian Wiccans also follow the three-stage initiation. In practice, although Sanders used a number of Gardner's innovations, he was less keen on Gardner's folkloric approach. Sanders promoted his own form of witchcraft now known as Alexandrian. However, modern-day witches see the Gardnerian and Alexandrian traditions as being similar in many respects. The major difference reflects Sander's partiality for

Alex Sanders had a flair for the dramatic and understood the power of the media.

ceremonial magical traditions. He incorporated elements of kabbala, Egyptian mythology and Hebrew magic in the form of Abra-Melin in his rituals. Ceremonial magic also gave him the opportunity to display his showmanship. He was often seen wearing dramatic robes, and also used impressive sounding incantations and exotic incense.

Starhawk (Miriam Simos) (1951–) – Spiral Dancer

Many have found their first introduction to Wicca in a book called *The Spiral Dance: A Rebirth of the Ancient Religion of the Great Goddess* (published in 1979). It was written by Miriam Simos, otherwise known as Starhawk. Following the Gardnerian traditional approach toward Wicca, Starhawk advocated the predominant worship of the goddess, and her reasoning reflected her strong interests in feminist principles. The goddess is linked to the earth mother, and Starhawk emphasized the celebration of nature as a celebration of the goddess.

Starhawk provided examples of the words and actions for ceremonies that noted the change of the season and the phases of the moon. The collection of eight celebrations, or Sabbats, are called the Wheel of the Year and are discussed in Chapter 6 (pages 124–35). They are an important element of Wiccan worship, designed to help the Wiccan align him- or herself to the mood of nature at each Sabbat. These ceremonies incorporate spells and affirmations specifically created for every sabbat. Starhawk described the Wheel of the Year as the search by the horned god of the goddess. Starhawk also advocates the freedom to create one's own sense of spirituality. This led her to further encourage Wiccans to make the time to understand themselves and others. Rituals are described by Starhawk as the creation of a collective energy which is directed by a leader who, in deep meditation, can focus the energy toward the purpose of the ritual.

PLACES OF MAGIC

EARTH MAGIC – TAPPING INTO THE EARTH'S ENERGY

A key element in raising energy to practice white magic is in understanding the mysteries of the earth. By aligning yourself with the earth's energy source, you will be able to bring the energy of the earth through your body and direct it toward the work you have in mind, without depleting yourself. It is equally important to "ground" or settle back into your body after a working by earthing the excess energy.

Grounding Exercises

One way to ground this energy is to take a piece of rock, crystal or stone and push it into the earth or floorboards, imagining that your energy is flowing back down through the body into the earth. Hematite and tiger iron are useful stones for grounding.

Another method is to sit comfortably on the floor or ground, close your eyes and visualize yourself as a tree. The first step is to concentrate on your spine as you are sitting, starting from the base and working vertebrae by vertebrae up to the base of your skull, helping you feel the flow of energy in your body. Imagine that your spine is bathed in a golden light. Focus on that light and see it flow along your spine, which is now transformed into the golden trunk of a tree. Imagine the base of your golden trunk extending downward into the earth. Let your mind drift free as you watch the roots grow and spread, stabilizing your body as they deepen.

Experiment with this image further, imagining branches rising up from the trunk and flowing gracefully in an arc-shape, like those of a willow tree, until they touch the ground. Feel the energy flow back to the roots.

To move out of the visualizations, focus on your breathing and, if you have used color, allow it to fade away. Open your eyes slowly. The feeling of being linked to the ground should continue with you for as long as you need to re-establish yourself into your body. Use this technique whenever you feel unsettled.

Sensing the Power – Using Your Intuition

Using your intuition to sense the power in the land around you is very important training for the working of magic. Some places are so strong that there is no question that there is a powerful increase of energy. This is particularly evident in places where there have been many centuries of worship, either pagan or Christian, or even nearby events of natural phenomena, such as earthquake zones and the sites of active volcanoes.

To further understand the earth's inherent magic, you will also be rewarded by the study of the art of dowsing, by understanding how ley lines work and why certain prominent sacred sites, such as Stonehenge, Avebury and Glastonbury in the United Kingdom, are concentrating spiritual energy. It is also worthwhile to visit less tourist-ridden ancient sites of worship so that you may have a chance to sense the power of the earth in peace and quiet. Sometimes a doorway is left open for those seeking enlightenment.

Dowsing — Seeking the Treasures of the Earth

Dowsers or water witches were particularly good at sensing where water could be found for farmers anxious to ensure that sinking a well would be rewarded with success. The dowser's tool was a forked twig, usually of hazel, which had been prepared under a waxing moon. Dowsing was also used for other divinatory purposes, such as the finding of lost property, treasure and even coal deposits. If the hazel was obtained at Midsummer Eve, it would be able to find buried treasure. However, in order for it to fulfill this purpose, German folklore stipulates that the hazel has to be prepared by being cut while its owner walks backward. To make sure the hazel has been prepared correctly, the wood should emit a squeal when it is brought close to water.

The practice of dowsing involves strong visualization skills. The dowser focuses his or her mind on the object of the search and walks over the suspected terrain, holding the dowsing rod by the forked ends in both hands, palms upward, waiting to feel a tug downward or certain vibrations that indicate the search is over. Dowsing can also be used for medical diagnosis, where it is more usual for a pendulum to be used over a chart of the body or the names of the vitamins and minerals that the body requires to be healed. A pendulum may be made by attaching a crystal or small piece of metal at the end of a string or thin chain.

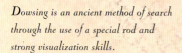

Dowsing is an ancient method of search through the use of a special rod and strong visualization skills.

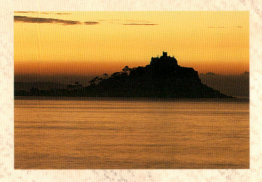

One of the longest ley lines in the United Kingdom starts at St. Michael's Mount in Cornwall.

Leys – Power Centers of the Earth

Leys are a network of energy lines surrounding the earth. A theory which was first put forward in 1925 was that the ancient civilizations understood the earth's energy field, building their sacred sites only at "ley centers". Leys appear to link these sacred sites with particular features of the earth, such as hills, mountain tops, wells, earthworks and the head of springs.

Ley centers, places where several ley lines intersect, have a heightened charge of energy. Modern ley hunters hypothesize that for a ley center to occur at least seven ley lines must intersect at that spot. The energy charge at ley centers can be classed as natural or artificial. An earthquake can create a natural charge whilst artificial charges can be created by the handling of stones which were to be used for the construction of the sacred site. The hammering and chiseling of the stones "fixes" the power. It is thought that the size of the stones and the number of blows required to shape each stone affected the power of the charge.

Sometimes the charge can be artificially induced by witches performing a ritual on site where they raise and direct psychic energy toward a stone. Experiments have found that the most effective rituals were those conducted during a full moon.

PROMINENT SACRED PLACES

Stonehenge — Link to the Cosmos?

Many questions remain about the purpose of Stonehenge, which was built between 3,500 to 1,100 B.C. in Wiltshire, England. A "henge" means a circular arrangement of stone and timber surrounded by a ditch or bank. Some of the stones at Stonehenge weigh more than 26 tons and measure over 20 feet (6.1 meters)in height. It has been calculated that the stone circle would have taken close to 1.5 million hours to build, given the absence of cranes and hydraulic power.

The purpose of Stonehenge is lost in the mists of history, but has attracted a variety of speculations. Excavations have shown that it was a burial site, and this discovery led to theories that an important personage, such as Boadicea, the famous pagan queen, was buried there. Some institutions, including the National Aeronautics and Space Administration, believe that Stonehenge is a link to the cosmos, either as a planetarium or a calculator of eclipses.

Avebury — the Largest Stone Circle in the World

Avebury is one of the largest stone circles in the world, covering over 28 acres (11.34 hectares). It consists of an outer circle of stones, some weighing over 60 tons, which is surrounded by a bank over 12 feet (3.66 meters) high. Originally, there were close to 100 stones in the outer circle, but now only 27 remain, the rest having been destroyed by people fearing or not respecting the power of the stones from as early as the fourteenth century. The toppled stones were then used for building in the village nestling within Avebury and some neighboring farms.

Like Stonehenge, Avebury's exact purpose is not known. Questions are still being asked whether Avebury was a burial site, cattle market, a sun temple or a Druidic serpent temple. Irrespective of Avebury's ancient purpose, the stones feel as if they have collected earth and psychic energy for many thousands of years. Avebury is known to have been in use between 2,600 and 1,600 B.C. and many traditions are still attached to its use — one of those concerns the young maidens of the village, who believe that their wishes will come true if they sit on the stone known as the Devil's Chair.

Stonehenge at Salisbury Plain, Wiltshire, continues to baffle experts. Some of the stones that make up the monument are believed to have come from Wales or parts of Ireland. Why stones in the immediate vicinity were not used remains a mystery.

Glastonbury – A Powerful Repository of Legends

Reputed to be the burial place of King Arthur, Glastonbury in Somerset, England, contains an enormous flow of energy that has attracted pagan and Christian worship through the centuries. A particularly powerful spot is Glastonbury Tor, which is a hill rising 500 feet (152.4 meters) made from volcanic rock and surmounted by the remains of a church tower dedicated to St. Michael. It has been speculated that Glastonbury was a Druidic sacred site and that there was a stone circle at its summit before the first Christian church was built on the site. The church on top of the Tor was rebuilt several times, once after a particularly destructive earthquake that caused a landslide on the Tor. A well, reputedly of magical water, lies at the Tor's base.

The energy of the Glastonbury has led it to become the repository of many powerful legends, such as it being the burial place of King Arthur and his queen, Guinevere; the hiding place of the Holy Grail; and the doorway to another world, either that of the fairies or extraterrestrials, depending on one's persuasions. Witches have held rituals on Glastonbury Tor, taking advantage of the indisputable power of the earth there. It is not surprising to learn that the Tor is also linked to Stonehenge and Avebury by two of the most significant leys in the south of England. It is curious that the ley starting from St. Michael's Mount in Cornwall connects many sites that are dedicated to St. Michael, including Glastonbury Tor.

Glastonbury Tor, depicted here in watercolor by Osmund Caine (living artist), is a sacred site of Druids, Christians and pagans alike.

CIRCLE MAGIC

Why a Circle?

The circle is a very powerful symbol. Some of the most important pagan spiritual sites, like Stonehenge and Avebury, have been in the form of a circle which is the symbol of infinity, unity, creation and the cycle of the seasons. Like our ancestors, modern witches and wizards believe that virtually all magic work should be conducted within a circle. By creating a Circle, you will be able to protect yourself from any harmful presences and concentrate the power that you are raising for your magic. Creating a Circle is a way of defining a safe space within which to link yourself into the earth, allowing you to use your space as a doorway to a higher power.

Finding Your Own Sacred Place

Before you can create a Circle, you will need to find a private space, either in nature or indoors, where you can practice your magic without distractions or interruptions. Your intuition will be your guide. If you live in the country, you may already know of a place with which you feel particularly attuned. If you choose to work outdoors, you will need to evaluate the safety of your area and how free it is from distractions. This is particularly important if you decide to work skyclad (naked).

If you live in the city, you may be lucky enough to be able to set aside a small room for your sacred place. It is surprising how soon a room like this becomes the heart of your home and helps you attune with nature despite the city noise around you.

Otherwise you may wish to set up your space near where you dream. While the traditional witch's Circle is nine feet (2.743 meters) in diameter, your Circle, if you wish to work by yourself, only needs to be large enough to encompass yourself and your altar.

Setting Up Your Own Sacred Place

One of the most important features in your sacred place is your altar. The altar represents the goddess, the earth mother, and is often set up facing north, particularly in the Northern Hemisphere. North corresponds with the element of earth. In the Southern Hemisphere, south corresponds with earth and most witches and wizards accordingly set their altars to the south.

On your altar it is important to have a number of tools that will help you touch the magic of the earth. First you will need tools that represent the four elements – earth, air, fire and water. For the proper flow of psychic energy you must pay attention to the combination of the four elements. You will need one of each of the following tools, which symbolize certain elements:

- ✪ **pentacle** made from clay or decorated onto a ceramic plate, a crystal or a stone ball to symbolize **earth**;
- ✪ **sword** or athame (small sharp knife) to symbolize **air**;
- ✪ **wand** that channels energy to symbolize **fire**; and
- ✪ **chalice** to symbolize **water**.

You will also need to mark out the elements around your Circle. There are many ways of doing this. Using a compass, quarter your Circle, so that at each spoke you can mark where each element falls. Your altar as a symbol of earth is already in either the north or the south, depending on the hemisphere in which you are working. Opposite your altar is the fire quarter. To your right, as you face the altar, is air and to your left is water.

A sunflower is an image that can be used to symbolize the earth quarter of your sacred place.

Depending on how permanent your space is, you may wish to decorate each quarter with appropriate symbols and colored candles.

For the air quarter, symbolizing your intellect, you may wish to decorate with branches (maybe those from an aspen tree), white candles and the images of birds. You could also consider placing your incense sticks or oil burner in this quarter. To decorate the fire quarter, symbolizing your will, you could try using red candles, images of the sun and plants suggestive of fire, such as sunflowers, marigolds or red peppers. Decorating the water quarter, symbolizing your emotions, can involve blue candles, images of the sea or river, mermaids, or a bowl of water with sea shells and some sand at the bottom topped by an aqua-blue floating candle. For the part of your altar set aside for the earth quarter, symbolizing your body, you can use brown or green candles or your favorite stones arranged in a circle, an earthware plate, images of fields or actual sheaves of wheat.

Apart from the elements, symbols for the god and goddess, or the Lord and the Lady, must also be set out. These symbols must be placed on the altar, the goddess on the left and god on the right. Appropriate symbols are candles — silver and gold are a good choice — or images or statues of your favorite god and goddess. Another possibility is placing objects you have found in nature on your altar that symbolize feminine and masculine qualities, such as the cowry shell for female energy and a crystal in the shape of a phallus for male energy.

It is important to use your own imagination, be guided by your own intuition and seek images that speak to your soul.

Casting and Closing a Circle

A Circle is thought to be a space between the worlds, a space where it is possible to direct your psychic energy for the good of your community. Before you cast your Circle you first need to purify your body and your space. For your own purification, it is an idea to have a ritual bath perfumed with your favorite essential oil and lit by a single candle. After bathing, if you are not working skyclad, be sure that whatever clothing you wear is spotlessly clean and is not used for everyday wear.

Back at your altar, sprinkle salt around your Circle space, while walking deosil (clockwise). When you are ready, sit quietly before your altar and concentrate on your breathing. One technique is to breathe in for a count of four and then out for a count of four. Continue this pattern until you feel a sense of stillness. You are now ready.

Stand up and take your athame from the altar. Starting in the air quarter, imagine at the tip of your outstretched athame a blue flame, which you trail as you slowly walk deosil around your sacred space. It is traditional to walk around your space three times, imagining the circle of blue flame growing into a blue-hued sphere.

Once cast, you should invite the elements and the Lady and the Lord (in that order) into your Circle. This, as well as a selection of spells and workings – rituals concentrated toward a specific purpose – will be discussed later in this book (*see* pages 58–61, 80 and 100). When you have finished your working, it is always good etiquette to thank the Lord and Lady and the elements for their presence within your Circle.

To close your Circle, walk widdershins (anti-clockwise), imagining that you are reeling in a blue cord. Once you are back to where you began, kneel down and imagine putting the cord back into the earth, along with all the energy that you had raised in your working. As a final step do the grounding exercises outlined on page 40.

SPELLCRAFT

WHAT ARE SPELLS AND HOW DO THEY WORK?

A spell is essentially a ritualized method of focusing the mind to help achieve a particular purpose. The key to spellcraft is to decide what you want to achieve by concentrating on the appropriate image or words. By the sheer act of concentration on what you wish, it could be said that you are opening an "astral doorway" to a new reality where what you want to bring into being will actually manifest. But your intention must be strong and consistent.

Aleister Crowley's most famous statement was: "Do what thou wilt shall be the whole of the Law". Many of his actions gave the impression that "do what thou wilt" meant that you can do anything you want. However, the key to this philosophy is to bring about a harmony between the conscious will and the often hidden purposes of one's higher self. To do this, you must be very clear in what you want. If not, your spellcraft will fail.

To aid concentration, traditions have evolved over the centuries concerning the images or words that are most effective for fulfilling certain goals, such as using red candles for a love spell. By linking into these traditions, you can sometimes help the spell to work because the procedures repeated over and over again seem to build up their own energy over time.

The Ethics of Spellcraft

In white magic, many of the spells that are cast are beneficial in purpose. It is important to remember the Wiccan phrase: "If it harm none, do what thou will". You must be careful when deciding what spell to cast that you do not act selfishly or try to hurt anyone. The danger in such practices are akin to the Eastern concept of karma, that whatever is sent out returns in time upon the sender. In Wicca, the formula is said to be "that which is sent out returns threefold".

Sometimes it is legitimate that a spell be worked to bind someone from doing harm to others. White witches have been known to work such magic when it is perceived to be for the greater good. However, there is always a price to be paid. During the Second World War, there were claims that British covens met to cast spells against Germany's invasion plans. Despite the worthiness of the spells, it was alleged that after one such ritual, several witches died as a consequence of the spells.

Underneath any exotic trappings, witches are no different to other people, and the spells cast by white witches are for beneficial purposes, not for sending harm to others.

Feeling Empowered — Sensing the Goddess Within

To cast a spell successfully, you must not only believe that the spell can work but also that you personally can make the change happen. Feeling empowered to make changes is one of the most important keys to being a witch or wizard. There are several techniques that can help you feel empowered. One such technique is to feel the presence of the goddess or the god within you and allowing the deity to act and speak through you.

When inviting the Lord and Lady to attend a Wiccan Circle, a very powerful process can be undertaken to really feel the presence of the Lady or the goddess called "Drawing down the Moon". Precisely how this is done varies from coven to coven and depends on a person's preference. Some say a special incantation while others may wish to invoke the goddess by standing in moonlight and imagining her energy reaching within them and enveloping them in a shimmering light. Whichever idea you choose to use, it is amazing how suddenly you feel your back straighten, your energy levels sharpen and your voice deepen. You become the goddess and through her you are able to direct your psychic energy more powerfully into your work.

Spellcraft Etiquette

To achieve a successful result through your spellcraft it is important to focus clearly on the outcome you want. You will, however, need to give yourself the time to think through the consequences of the spell. If you are contemplating a healing spell, make sure your patient really wants to be well. There is a theory that people become sick for a particular karmic purpose, and you may need to use your intuition to work out whether you would be interfering with your patient's own true will. Also it is useful in a healing spell to first ask your patient for his or her permission to work a spell on his or her behalf. It can aid a working, if the patient is aware of when you are going to cast the spell — he or she can then prepare themselves to be open for the healing. Sharing the images and wording of the ritual can help.

It is advisable, unless in dire circumstances, always to ask the permission of the person involved before casting any spell, since otherwise the recipient of your best intentions may feel that his or her privacy has been invaded. Love spells too should be approached with caution. It is acceptable to ask for a glimpse at one's future lover, but it is not ethical to make someone fall in love with you or anyone else using spellcraft. This type of spellcraft can easily be categorized as black magic because you are tampering with a person's free will.

As a final word, whenever you have gained the result you wish through spellcraft, it is always polite to thank the Lord and the Lady and any other entity that you linked into for the success of your spell for their help in achieving your goal. You may wish to set aside some wine and a piece of cake, which can be offered to the Lord and the Lady after your ritual is complete.

Opposite: The Lord and the Lady must be thanked after the working of your spell. To do this, take some wine and cake into the garden or to some patch of earth and thank the Lord and Lady as you place your offerings into the ground.

VISUALIZATION

Making It Happen

Concerning the practice of spellcraft, we have discussed the importance of focusing your will, of being confident in your power, and of weighing the merits of your action. To take it one step further, you now need to imagine the success of your spell as if it had already worked. If you cast a spell for getting a new job, for instance, imagine sitting in a new office with a healthy pay check in the drawer. Imagine everything about the office, even the woodgrain on the desk, and visualize how you look and feel in that new environment, specifically, imagine the feeling of success.

Getting into the Mood –
Some Visualization Exercises

If your mind starts to wander when you are trying to visualize the success of your project, it might be worthwhile to do a few visualization exercises to help you concentrate. If the spell is for yourself, it is possible you are subconsciously sabotaging your spell by feeling in some way unworthy of success.

Take the time to understand any misgivings you may have about the success you seek. If you are not a hundred per cent behind your spell, it is unlikely to work. This is sometimes why even experienced witches ask another in their coven or acquaintance to do the spell for them.

Visualization exercises are simple but do take a great deal of concentration and perseverance. Take the time to try out the following two exercises as they are well worth practicing:

⊛ Try focusing on a photograph of a landscape, noticing all the details in the photograph, such as the shape of the trees. Once you feel confident that you know the picture well, tear the photograph in half. Put one half on the table in front of you and try to visualize the other half.

⊛ An advanced exercise is to try visualizing a piece of fruit. Use all your senses — see the fruit, touch it, smell it and eat it, hear the crunch as you bite into it.

Flying Your Broomstick — An Exercise in Visualization?

One of the more extravagant accusations traditionally aimed at witches was that they could fly on a broomstick. Invariably there were all manner of disgusting ointments which presumably gave witches the ability to fly. Many of them seemed to have copious amounts of puppy or baby fat and a dash of henbane or belladonna. Was there any truth in this myth?

In one sense it is highly unlikely that people could levitate on a broomstick and fly through the night. But in another sense a witch or wizard can easily visualize flying and visiting specific people. A very experienced witch or wizard could go one step further and project his or her spirit, or astral body, and fly in real time to where he or she wished to go. This is otherwise known as astral projection. Astral projection is a very advanced technique and one that should not be attempted by someone starting out in magic, because it is often difficult to ground afterward.

The flying ointment of folk tradition may have assisted the witch in feeling she could fly since several recipes contained hallucinogenic agents that could be absorbed through the skin. And why the broomstick? This is still under speculation. Theories range from the broomstick being a convenient implement lying around the house to it being linked to fertility rites.

MAKING AND USING YOUR MAGICAL TOOLS

Combining the Elements

While the first few steps to proper spellcraft include having belief in yourself and a clear intention, the next step is to achieve what Wiccans call an "elemental balance". In many traditions, to perform magic a person must be equally attuned to the elements of earth, air, fire and water in their personality and their lifestyle. This is reflected in the possession, by a witch or wizard, of four important ritual tools representing each element, the pentacle (earth), the athame (air), the wand (fire) and the chalice (water).

It is essential that anyone attempting to practice magic is themselves as balanced as he or she can be. There is always a danger in magic that if a person has not resolved his or her own particular problems and has not achieved some form of balance between his or her intellect (air), will (fire), emotions (water) and body (earth), he or she may find it difficult to raise and control the energy for spellcraft. Should you find any such imbalance in your own psychic make-up or even lifestyle, work with the particular element you have diagnosed as weak within yourself until you are able to create balance within yourself; for instance, if your will is weak, work with images of fire to strengthen your resolve. This will be of benefit to you not only within spellcraft but in all aspects of life.

One way of working with an element for achieving balance is to actually make the tool that corresponds with that element. There is something very special about having tools that you have made yourself or have commissioned a craftsman to make for you. In the following pages we will look at some ideas for making or acquiring your own magical tools, with a glance at some of the pitfalls which you can easily avoid.

The Altar and your tools must always be kept clean.
When the Altar is not in use you may carefully store
your tools away from inquisitive hands. When visiting the
Altar of another Witch, it is good manners to ask permission
before you touch anything on the Altar.

Making Your Magical Tools

Athame (Air)

△

A double-edged knife called the athame is one of the most important tools in the practice of white magic. The handle of this knife is usually black and the blade may be made of steel or stone, such as obsidian. Iron is to be avoided. Experiment with how the shape of the handle fits in your hand.

Ideally, if you can, you should make your own athame. If you do, remember that in its making you should expose the knife to all the elements — pass it through fire, immerse it in water, plunge into the earth, and expose it to the air. If you decide to buy a knife from a store, you can make it more personal by attaching leather, some feathers and beads.

Athames are used to cast a Circle and symbolize male energy.

Wand (Fire)

△

A magical wand is made from wood and there are traditions as to what is the best wood for wands — ash is a popular choice. Wood that is struck from its tree by lightning is known to be particularly potent.

You may find your wand anywhere from a hardware store to a forest. A broken branch from a tree in your favorite place can be whittled down. However, it is important that you *do not pull branches off trees as this will create bad energy.*

The size of your wand is a matter of preference, although a convenient and traditional length is 21 inches (53 cm). Your wand can be decorated with runes or a dragon carved along the length of the wand with head and teeth at the tip.

The wand is used to direct magical energy in a ritual.

Chalice (Water)

There is a tradition that you must be given your own chalice. Chalices can be made from pewter, glass or any other watertight material. Because of their nature, chalices tend to be store bought but you may know of a glassblower who could craft a chalice for you, perhaps with swirls of blue and green.

A chalice is representative of female energy. Most Circles include, before closing, a small ceremony called "wine and cakes". The wine and food must be blessed before partaking. Your chalice may be used for the wine. By dipping your athame into your chalice you are blessing the wine.

Pentacle (Earth)

Made of clay, metal or wood, the pentacle represents the earth element. The shape of the pentacle must be circular and can either be a flat disc, such as a ceramic plate, or a sphere, such as a stone or crystal ball. Balls of jasper, hematite and tiger's eye (which contains iron), just to name a few, are thought to be particularly powerful. If you wish to decorate your disc or ball, the sign of the pentagram is appropriate.

The pentagram is a five-pointed star. In white magic the point of the star is always at the top, representing life. To draw the star, start from the top and move down to the left and follow the pattern shown here. If your pentacle is a plate, it may be used in the wine and cakes ceremony to hold the food over which you make the sign of the pentagram as a sign of blessing.

To draw your pentagram start at the top and follow the arrows.

SPELLS

Preparing for Your Spell

It is preferable, for the success of the spell, that you cast it within the safety of your own Circle in your own sacred space. There you will be able to utilize the power of the Lord and Lady as well as the elements. Surrounded by your magical tools, you will be aided in your spell by their inherent power.

It is also useful to time the casting of your spell according to the moon's phases. In many traditions, during the waxing of the moon, all positive spells, such as those for love and healing, need to be cast. Full moon is one of the most effective times to do any type of magic. Negative spells are done during the waning of the moon, with the most potent time being close to new moon. Negative magic includes binding spells and is basically the time to cast out unwanted habits or end disruptive relationships.

When practicing spellcraft, carefully choose what tools and materials you are going to use for your working. These are essentially props designed to help you visualize your goal. You may wish to use wax, for instance, to shape an image of the person for whom you wish to do a healing spell. Wax was often used by witches in the days of persecution, so that if interrupted, they could return the image easily to a plain ball of wax. It is always preferable to use materials that are as close to nature as possible, such as cotton, silk and beeswax, rather than artificially created materials because, according to tradition, they are able to hold psychic energy better. Gather your tools and materials on your altar and check carefully that you have everything you need. Any interruptions will impede the flow of energy.

CHANTS

How Do Chants Work?

The power of the human voice and the creation of sound vibrations can add enormously to the raising of psychic power aimed at a particular purpose. Chanting your spell can heighten its intensity, with repetition being highly effective in concentrating your focus and leading you into an altered state of consciousness. Mantras, which are the repetition of a word or phrase, are often used in Eastern religions to aid meditation. Chanting is in effect a kind of breath control.

Group chanting is particularly invigorating. One person usually leads the chant and supervises to make sure that all participants feel they are tuning into the group purpose. Almost of its own accord, the group energy will eventually start to build. The leader will feel when the energy is about to peak, and then, by a pre-determined gesture, the leader will signal that the chant should end with a last push of air, effectively releasing the group's energy. Silence falls as all return to their normal rate of breathing.

You do not have to learn any special words to be able to do a chant. One technique is to use either a humming sound or any syllables that pop into your head as you are chanting. These are called wordless chants. For the Buddhists, chanting the word "OM" will be enough to help balance the body and the spirit. Some traditions have incorporated the singing of particular sounds to awaken the seven chakras in your body. It is believed that once the chakras, or energy points rising along the center of your body, are awakened, energy will flow smoothly from the base of the spine to the crown of the head.

Through the power of cord spellcraft, webs of magic can be woven.

USING CORD MAGIC

S ome of the most effective spells use cord magic. For this type of magic you need a length of rope or cord into which you can knot your intentions or will. With all spells, it is important that once you have finished the actual casting you must leave the spells alone to do their work. Cord magic makes it easier for you to leave the knotted rope in a special place or box with your intentions firmly contained within the rope.

How many knots should you use? There are some numbers that seem always to crop up in magic, such as the number 3 and its multiples. The number 9 is thought to be particularly magical. In medieval times it was considered the foremost angelic number and numerically any number multiplied by 9 would also add up to 9. You can further intensify your aim by using suitably colored cords, such as red for love and green for money.

The following spell is a traditional one, noted in several texts on magic. It incorporates cord magic and the magic number 9. Try it. You need to first state out loud what your aim is, for instance, a new job. With a cord long enough to be knotted 9 times, say the following words and make the knots in the following pattern, still concentrating on the successful outcome of your desire:

By knot of one, the spell's begun.

◎ —————————————

By knot of two, it cometh true.

◎ ——————————————— ◎

By knot of three, so mote it be.

◎ ——————— ◎ ——————— ◎

By knot of four, power I store.

◎ —— ◎ —— ◎ —— ◎

By knot of five, the spell is alive.

◎ —— ◎ —— ◎ —— ◎ —— ◎

By knot of six, the spell is fixed.

◎ – ◎ – ◎ – ◎ – ◎ –◎

By knot of seven, events I'll leaven.

◎ – ◎ – ◎ – ◎ – ◎ – ◎ –◎

By knot of eight, it will be Fate.

◎ – ◎ – ◎ – ◎ – ◎ – ◎ – ◎ –◎

By knot of nine, what is done is mine.

◎ – ◎ – ◎ – ◎ – ◎ – ◎ – ◎ – ◎ –◎

CANDLE MAGIC

How Does Candle Magic Work?

Primarily candle magic involves choosing a candle of the appropriate color for the purpose of your work. Candles of different colors can be prepared to represent certain things, such as those indicated by the table below:

Red — sexual love, strength, high energy
Pink — affectionate love
Orange — openness, flexibility
Yellow/Gold — confidence, charm
Green — money, fertility
Blue — patience, health
Purple — ambition, power

Once you have chosen the appropriate candle, you will need to prepare it. First, you may wish to choose a compatible oil, such as patchouli oil for a red love candle, and rub the oil into the candle. Choose oils that you associate with your purpose. If in doubt, use a neutral carrier oil, such as almond oil. This is called anointing the candle. In one tradition, the candle must be rubbed from the center outward while concentrating on the purpose you wish to achieve. Olive oil is a good substitute if you do not have access to aromatherapy essential oils.

The candle may also have its purpose carved down its side in either your mother tongue or a magical alphabet, such as runes. Set up your Circle as described on page 48 and then place your candle onto or into a safe receptacle, such as a small cauldron half-filled with sand to catch the falling wax. During your Circle, focus on your will, look into the flame and "see" the successful outcome of your will. Pour this energy into the candle. At this stage you can either extinguish the candle or leave it in the cauldron to burn itself out. If you do extinguish the candle before closing your Circle, you can watch the smoke rise from the wick and imagine that your spell is intermingling with reality, already changing Fate according to your will.

The light of a candle is used to honor the Lord and Lady, the Elements and the intention of your spell.

MANIFESTING MAGICAL POWER

Consecrating Magical Power

To consecrate means to dedicate or make sacred a tool, a piece of ritual jewelry, a talisman or an amulet. When you have made or have finished decorating the tools you wish to use they will require consecration. You can do this by "presenting" the object to all the four elements by sprinkling the object with salted water (water), passing it through a flame (fire) and incense smoke (air) and then sprinkling earth over it (earth).

Crosses

In pagan times, crosses were associated with sun gods and the heavens. As such, they have been used for many centuries predating Christianity as powerful wards against evil spirits. There are a number of different types of crosses. A popular pagan cross is the equal-armed cross which, when enclosed in a circle, is symbolic of each of the elements. The T-shaped cross adopted by the Christian Church became more than an amulet, it became a symbol of the death and resurrection of Christ.

Where energy, in the form of contemplation, prayers and meditation, has been consistently focused on a particular symbol, it is thought that the symbol itself develops a powerful energy field. Many believe that nothing evil can withstand the power of the Christian cross. Victims of demonic possession and vampires were supposed to be repelled by its image and the Inquisitors wore crosses when interrogating alleged witches.

Amulets

An amulet is a protective device worn either on the body or placed at the entrances of homes and tombs and can take the form of an image or a symbol. The Egyptian ankh, the cross and the Star of David are all used as amulet designs. The Roman philosopher Pliny described three types of amulets — protective amulets, those used for the treatment of illnesses, and those containing medicinal substances. Abbess Hildegarde of Bingen had a recipe for an amulet to protect the wearer from poison, which involved drying out the heart of a venomous snake, the remains of which could be worn in a small container around the neck. In white magic, the most powerful amulet is the five-pointed star — the pentagram, with one tip pointing upwards.

Talismans

It is thought that the words or sigils used on talismans set up a delicate vibration that serve to help its wearer attain special powers. Sigils — a special sign that incorporates a form of magical energy — include a design or image intended to symbolize a deity or a magical concept and they served as a focus for calling upon that deity or spirit. Sigils may be used as amulets or as talismans.

Unlike amulets, which passively protect its wearer, talismans contain supernatural powers that confer special powers to the wearer, such as clairvoyance or the power to make fortunes. The most famous talisman was the Philosopher's Stone, which allegedly could cure all illness and turn base metals into gold.

Fetishes, Voodoo Dolls and Poppets

A fetish is generally any object that has magical power, including wooden dolls, teeth, stones or bones. Fetishes could be used for either healing or malignant purposes.

Voodoo dolls gained notoriety when used for destructive magic. The image of a person is made and then struck through with knives, nails or pins, each stab intensifying the pain for the intended victim. However, dolls can be used for white magic and in this case are sometimes known as poppets.

A poppet can be used for healing and for finding the perfect partner. In some traditions a poppet is prepared in your special Circle space. You will need natural cloth (calico is ideal) from which to cut out two identical outlines of a figure. These should be sewn together, leaving the top of the head open. Turn the figure inside out, or if you are good at blanket stitch, sew around the edges of the cloth. Through the top of the head, stuff the figure with the appropriate herbs. If you are doing a love spell, say to attract your perfect partner, use herbs that are said to be ruled by Venus, such as vervain, rosebuds or yarrow. See pages 82 – 87 for herbs suitable for healing a particular illness or discomfort.

As you are making these preparations concentrate on what type of person you wish to attract or the person you wish to heal. Consecrate the poppet (*see* Consecrating Magical Power, page 68) and focus all your energy into your will.

In white magic poppets are used for healing and good fortune. Any harm sent out through a poppet used as a voodoo doll, will be returned threefold.

Charms

Charms are magical words or chants used to ward off evil or undesirable circumstances. A charm can also be a prayer. There have been charms since ancient times dealing with many contingencies, the most common being for health and love. Many charms exist in verbal form, their phrases or verses handed down, with variations, through folklore. The following charm was very popular for revealing your future lover:

> Good St. Thomas, do me right
> And bring my love to me this night,
> That I do look him in the face
> And in my arms may him embrace.

Often charms are accompanied by certain ritualized actions, such as spitting or wrapping onion peel in linen. Some of the charms that have come down to us through the ages are hard to verify because the actions that are required to accompany the words are virtually impossible to fulfill, such as standing under a certain tree on a certain night waiting for the first seed to fall, presumably without shaking the tree in frustration.

Sometimes charms are said while making preparations for Circle work, particularly if gathering fresh herbs for a healing spell. You can make up your own words, asking the herbs to release their most potent energy to help in the healing. If you are able to make the words rhyme, it will be more powerful and, of course, easier to remember. For an example of a charm that could be said whilst gathering herbs for a healing spell, *see* page 83.

Charms can also be written down on parchment or wood and worn around the neck in a decorative container, preferably with a secret catch. Charms can also be incorporated as part of an amulet, such as the phrase "Abracadabra" which was thought to have first started out as a cure for fever. Amulets with inscriptions are often called charms.

RECORDING YOUR MAGICAL EXPERIENCES

Keeping a Personal Magical Journal

It is very important that you record your experiences and insights in a journal while doing Circle work. Bring your journal to Circle, keeping it near your altar, so that if a particular image comes to you during Circle you can, in the quiet time before its closing, write down your impressions while they are still fresh. You then still have the advantage of being in your sacred Circle space so that you can still ask for clarification if there is something you do not understand.

It often happens that after a magical working, your dreams are particularly vivid. If you had requested guidance on, say, your path in life, you may find that your answer may not come during the Circle but will appear in your dreams. Keep your magical journal beside your bed or, if you wish, keep a separate journal especially for noting your dreams.

Book of Shadows – Honoring the Secrets of Others

As noted in Chapter 1, modern-day witchcraft was largely inspired by a work of Gerald Gardner's called *Book of Shadows*. Subsequent versions were revised by Gardner and Doreen Valiente and have been the workbook of a number of covens and the basis of a number of traditions. People actually initiated into the Craft are sometimes required to hand copy his or her initiator's personal Book of Shadows. In other traditions, it is thought best to develop your own Book of Shadows.

Throughout the 1950s and 1960s, reference to a Book of Shadows was usually the Gardnerian work. Today virtually each witch or wizard has a personal Book with magical practices, wordings and images from a vast range of religious systems and beliefs. It is "Craft" etiquette to only reveal your initiator's Book of Shadows to someone with your initiator's permission.

Grimoires – A Cautionary Tale: Are You Ready?

There have been many exotic tales spoken and written of the search for an ancient grimoire that contains the secret to everlasting life, fortune and other dangerous powers. A grimoire is a book that is a compilation of a number of spells, techniques and mysteries used over a period of time (see Chapter 5, page 108 for an outline of the most famous grimoires). The tales generally conclude with the person who found the grimoire being unable to handle the power unleashed by the ancient text. Similarly, in magic, it is understood that certain magical practices or rituals are to be attempted only by those who have sufficient magical training. In some magical systems, a hierarchy of levels is developed so that a person will have goals in developing his or her skills.

Another Cautionary Tale

There have been instances where people have attempted magic too advanced for their experience and they suffered for their mistake. Calling down ancient spirits to do your bidding is a notoriously risky pastime. Attempting rituals that are deemed to be of a certain level without having built up your skills through the less demanding levels can leave you drained, not just for a few hours or a few days, but for years. So be careful and always remember, you often get what you ask for, whether you like it or not.

THE WITCH'S WORLD

KITCHEN WITCH OR PAGAN GODDESS?

A modern-day witch can be whoever she wants to be and practice whatever form of magic she finds suitable for her. However, the overall common denominators among witches is the belief in the balance of female and male energies and the acceptance of the elevation of the goddess to the status of equal worship with the god. Some witches worship the goddess exclusively. For the purpose of this book we have divided magical practices between kitchen witch and ceremonial magician, although if so inclined or deemed necessary, the so-called kitchen witch may also practice ceremonial magic.

The kitchen witch usually lives her life by observing the magic of nature, feeling the seasons through the food she prepares to nurture her body and soul, and to nurture the needs of others through the tending of her garden and the blessings she bestows upon her own house and the houses of others. She may inspire and help hurt souls who need guidance and reassurance, carrying with her always stones, special herbs or flower essences that help soothe and provide insight or give protection.

To make the magic powerful and to help her practice her magic with clarity and insight, a kitchen witch will tap into the great feminine energy. She may call it simply "the Lady" or she may feel affinity with a goddess of a particular culture or tradition.

She will ask for guidance under the shimmering light of the full moon, draw into herself the energy of the moon and feel from within the power of the goddess. She will meditate in front of the flame of a single candle to ground herself and become part of the earth, or dance and chant to invoke a fierce energy directed at stopping the earth's destruction. She is kitchen witch and she is goddess.

POPULAR PAGAN GODDESSES

There are a bewildering range of goddesses from a myriad of cultures, both past and present, into whose power the modern witch can tap. In every culture there is usually a female entity who is the wife or mother of the predominent god figure.

In Egyptian mythology, she is known as Isis, while in Norse mythology she is known as Frigg and Freya. In almost every culture there is the same vision of Mother Earth and the creation and sustenance of life, both physical and spiritual. In Wicca, the goddess has three main aspects — the Maid, the Mother and the Crone. The "Triple Goddess" represents the cyclic nature of life, which can be seen in the phases of the moon — the Maid being represented by the new moon, the Mother by the full moon, and the Crone by the waning or dark moon.

The Lady — Mother of the Gods

"The Lady" is a name for the main current of feminine energy. It is useful to take some time to feel her presence while in Circle and to see her in her different guises. As an example, you may feel her presence at new moon as playful or joyful, filling you with a sense of lightness and hope. At full moon you may see her as a mature woman, guiding your steps and nurturing your soul. At waning moon, you may see her as the wise old woman who shows you a path through the darkness.

As you concentrate, you may start to visualize a female entity with an energy that may help you balance your life, for instance the Celtic mother goddess, Brigid, may come to you if you are feeling victimized. Your goddess may not tell you her name, but you will find clues from her garments, jewelry or companion animal.

Isis — Queen of Heaven

Isis is the Egyptian version of a mother goddess, to whom all aspects of civilized life is often attributed, such as the creation of a justice system. It was believed by the Egyptians that from her sprang all the other gods and goddesses. She is said to be known by 10,000 names, including Regina Coeli and the Queen of Heaven, and many occult traditions equate her with the Virgin Mary. She is also the goddess of sailing and was known as the *Stella Maris* (Star of the Sea) in Greek and Roman cultures.

Her image was revived during the late nineteenth century, as were many other aspects of Egyptian spiritual practices. The first temple of the Hermetic Order of the Golden Dawn was called Isis-Urania and Madame Blavatsky's first book was called *Isis Unveiled* (see Chapter 1, page 35). In Hermeticism, Isis was thought to have been the daughter of Hermes and came to be the symbol of wisdom, truth and power, being particularly associated with healing magic. Her healing powers are linked to her role in revitalizing her brother-husband Osiris, who had been murdered and dismembered by his jealous brother Set. She also acquired her immortality, being formerly a mortal magician, by tricking the Egyptian sun god Ra to reveal his secret name.

In the twentieth century, the Fellowship of Isis was founded in Ireland where Isis and Osiris are venerated as the goddess and god. The Fellowship is a religion that aims to encourage compassion, the development of psychic skills and reverence of the feminine aspects of spirituality, as well as an appreciation of love, beauty and abundance. Education programs are also available to Fellowship members to help them chart their spiritual development through 33 "degrees" — the name of each set stage of development.

A bronze votive statuette of Isis and her child Horus seated on a wooden throne and base (c.664 – 332 B.C.) was found at the Saqqarah Step Pyramid in Egypt.

Diana the Huntress, *by Gaston Casimir Saintpierre (1833 – 1916)*.

Diana

Diana is the goddess of the moon and the hunt in Roman mythology and is popular in British myth. Her equivalent in Greek mythology is Artemis. She represents new moon and the moon in the waxing phase as she is the virgin goddess, as yet beholden to no man. New beginnings and the achievement of goals are her domain. The two other goddesses who traditionally represent the moon in its full stage are Selene and, in its dark aspect, Hecate. Although Diana is a moon goddess, she walks the earth and is associated with wild woods and animals. In the Middle Ages, with the surge of the Christian faith, Diana became reviled as a demon and the patroness of evil, turning women's minds away from being faithful and dutiful.

Diana is representative of independence and confidence and is one of the many patron goddesses of witches. She is the usual goddess that women, either in childbirth or in victimized situations, pray to for help. In modern witchcraft there are now feminist covens who revere Diana in her aspect as goddess of the moon and the nurturer and protector of women. These covens practice what is known as Dianic witchcraft which, unlike most forms of Wicca, exclusively worships the goddess.

Aradia

In Italian lore, Aradia, an earth goddess, was the daughter of Diana and Lucifer, who was given the mission of teaching witches their Craft. The story of Aradia was first published in the late nineteenth century by Charles Godfrey Leland, an American who studied the oral traditions of folklore in Italy. The story of Aradia was allegedly told to him by an hereditary Tuscan witch called Maddalena, but he also referred to a supposedly ancient manuscript, which he had obtained, called *Aradia, or the Gospel of the Witches.*

The manuscript gave the origins of Aradia and stated that her aims were to teach witches how to hit back against their persecutors with the use of poisons and the perpetration of other malicious acts. There were also references to the celebration of Esbats or full-moon rituals that involved dancing, singing and making love under the full moon. Gerald Gardner was very taken by the story of Aradia and refers to her as the goddess in his *Book of Shadows.* Aradia is sometimes invoked by modern witches, mainly as a moon goddess. Once invoked, the goddess is said to give a charge or address to the members of the coven through the high priestess. The wording of that charge has, in some traditions, been adapted from Leland's book.

INVOKING THE GODDESS

To invoke the goddess means to invite her to be present in your Circle. A goddess is traditionally invoked by being drawn into the person conducting the Circle, in some traditions called the high priestess. This part of Circle work is called "Drawing down the Moon". If you work magic by yourself, known as working solitary, see Chapter 3 (page 54) for a description of how to invite the goddess into your Circle.

Drawing down the Moon

The invocation of Drawing down the Moon is one of the most powerful experiences that a witch can have. The moon is equated with the goddess, and by focusing on the light of the moon and feeling it shine through your body, you will feel the energy of the goddess within you. The process of Drawing down the Moon can be stimulated by the use of a particular goddess's name or a number of goddesses' names and by visual images of the goddess.

Witches since classical times were thought to be able to control the moon and draw her power down to do their bidding. In some traditions, where a modern coven seeks to Draw down the Moon, the high priestess meditates upon the goddess and may allow herself to fall into a trance to prepare for the high priest's invocation of the goddess into the high priestess. From that point of the Circle, the high priestess becomes the channel for the goddess. How much of a channel becomes evident when the high priestess delivers her charge. A charge is an address to the other participants of the ritual. The charge can be the standard one used by many covens that was written by Gerald Gardner and revised by Doreen Valiente. However, sometimes the goddess has been channeled strongly and the words of the charge come *through* the high priestess, not *from* her.

Working with a Particular Goddess

When working with herbs or natural objects, you may wish to link into the fertile, creative goddess energy, personified as the earth mother. The earth mother seeks balance in the world and it is through the use of herbs, healing plants the earth mother has nurtured, that you seek to balance a person's health, and through divination that you seek to balance a person's psyche.

You may wish to work with a goddess from a particular culture. The first step is to know as much as you can about her, especially her likes and dislikes. There might also be information about how she was worshiped and for what she was revered. Often, in order to attract the benevolence of the goddess, altars and temples were built and decorated with certain symbols.

Be specific about which aspect of the goddess you wish to invoke or work with. It is important to remember that many goddesses, including the earth mother, have their dark side. In witchcraft there is no dichotomy between good and evil. There is no such thing as the Devil. Instead, there is a balance in the earth mother between creativity and death, symbolized in the cycle of the seasons and the phases of the moon.

KITCHEN WITCHCRAFT

We have attributed to the kitchen witch skills in healing, blessings and divination that use plant forms and other natural objects, such as stones, especially semi-precious ones. Working with natural objects includes observing the cycles and the vibrations involved in their use. The witch must learn the times, seasons and phases of the moon when particular herbs should be cut. When using other natural objects such as stones, she will always purify them before use by cleansing them with salty water.

Working with Herbs

How often have we seen images of witches cackling over a bubbling cauldron, asking a colleague for a dash of Swine Snout. It is often not remembered that herbs have many names, the most definitive being their Latin name. Swine Snout is otherwise known as dandelion (*Taraxacum dens leonis*).

Herbs could be used not only for healing but for protection, consecration of particular ritual tools, fertility, visions and even immortality. The correct preparation of herbs is essential for enhancing their healing properties. Growing herbs is easy, because they generally do not need particularly good soil and they respond well to companion planting, that is planting certain flowers, herbs and vegetables together, which help each other grow.

Herbs need to be cut when the day is dry and hung on string in a dry room. Folkloric traditions recommend cutting herbs at full moon to bring health, and at waning to new moon to cure disease. If you wish to use herbs to assure the beginning of a new project, cut them at new moon. Better results are achieved if a small sickle or boline, a consecrated white-handled knife, is reserved solely for this cutting.

Incorporating Herbs into Your Spells

There are a number of ways of directing and enhancing the power of the herbs for your healing spell. Small chants can be said while cutting the herbs for a particular purpose or person. A simple line or two, or a small verse like the one below, will help focus your mind and align your thoughts with your intention:

> *In thee, small plant, doth magic live,*
> *By sun and rain and earth made whole;*
> *I conjure thee thy power to give*
> *To heal the flesh, to ease the soul.*

If you wish to be able to prescribe home-cut herbs for internal intake and poultices, it would be wise to make a serious study of herbs and their properties, as well as a study of anatomy and physiology. Many of the herbs you will be using are not dangerous, but if you do not know the properties of herbs sufficiently, you may become discouraged if the effect you seek does not eventuate. You can end up using too much of your own energy trying to make the herb do what it was not designed to do. For example, do not use valerian for anything other than relaxing the body. Witches are often rewarded well when they become attuned with what nature offers them.

There are ways, however, of using dried herbs other than for internal use. The smell of herbs can in itself be beneficial to calm, balance and protect a person from illness. One idea is to make a little herb sachet that can be hung around your patient's neck, allowing the warmth, particularly between the breasts, to release the fragrance. A small bag can be made out of a circle of leather or silk and a thong threaded around the circumference. Knot the ends of the thong and pull the circle into a small bag within which you can pop a muslin bag with the appropriate herb or mix of herbs and a little blessing, perhaps written on a piece of parchment. A small semi-precious stone can also be included.

Popular Herbs for Magical Purposes

For a full description of the properties of herbs, it might be useful to purchase a good herbal, such as Dr. Nicholas Culpeper's *Complete Herbal*. Although Dr. Culpeper was a herbalist and astrologer in the early seventeenth century, his herbal is still considered a good reference work.

There have been, through the ages, many alleged secret potions that were brewed for a number of desired outcomes, including immortality. The herb chervil was thought to be the herb of immortality, and dragon's blood was believed to help those wishing to learn astral traveling or to safeguard secret documents.

Certain herbs are more effective when made up as amulets. St. John's Wort is a great herb for protection and, if you wish to make an amulet containing it, it should be gathered during midsummer. Likewise, little oak acorns can be made into amulets, representing fertility and bringing to fruition your own creativity, and a piece of cedar carried in your wallet or purse will attract money. When you have finished making your amulet, consider sprinkling some chamomile into it as the herb is renown for its promise of success. If you are seeking good luck, make an amulet containing cinnamon. For love potions, clover can be used to find out who your soul mate will be. For the protection of your family, cumin could also be added to your amulet.

Many celebrations are conducted during a Wiccan year, including the eight sabbats representing the Wheel of the Year (*see* Chapter 6). At these time it is usual for food to be prepared to celebrate the particular season. Many of the herbs can be used within sabbat dishes to heighten the mood of the season. Tarragon can be included to help your guests feel compassionate and nurturing, and savory is a useful herb for generating a feeling of joy and happiness, while cloves engender a feeling of kinship. This table of the properties contained within each herb will help you choose the right herb for your dish or magical spell.

TABLE OF MAGICAL HERBS

Herb	Properties
Acorn	aids success in creative work
Agrimony	aids psychic healing, aura cleansing
Angelica	protects against psychic attack
Basil	gives courage before initiation
Borage	promotes happiness and joy
Camphor	cleanses and purifies
Chamomile	calms and protects
Chervil	promotes wisdom
Cinnamon	aids concentration and focus
Coriander	brings immortality, peace
Cucumber	increases psychic ability and intuition
Dill	dispels negative energies
Dogwood	aids in keeping secrets
Dragon's Blood	protects, used to seal sacred manuscripts
Fennel	protects, aids ability to face danger and adversity
Frankincense	protects, cleanses, and aids concentration
Garlic	protects, enhances power of strength
Ginger	protects
Hemp	useful for anointing tool of divination
Honeysuckle	aids understanding of the mysteries
Horehound	aids trust in your intuition
Hyssop	protects, particularly the house
Jasmine	gives psychic protection
Lavender	increases awareness
Lovage	draws romance into one's life
Mistletoe	is protective, brings harmony
Mugwort	promotes inner enlightenment
Myrrh	heightens magical awareness
Parsley	heightens communion with mother earth
Peppermint	improves divination skills
Sage	promotes wisdom and cleanses evil
Valerian	protects and cleanses
Verbena	enhances lucid dreaming

HOUSE BLESSINGS

Dispersing Negative Energies

House blessings are an important feature of a kitchen witch's work. There are two stages to a house blessing. First you need to cleanse the house of any negative energies that have stayed within its walls. These energies may be sensed if you get a feeling of being, at the very least, slightly uncomfortable in the house or some part of it. Use your intuition. The second stage is to set up a protective energy around the house, sealing all the openings with the sign of the pentagram or an appropriate protective herb mixed with salted water.

Tools You Will Need

You will need your athame or a consecrated knife and a candle. As the first stage of the house blessing is a cleansing ritual you may choose to use a white candle. You may also wish to prepare some herbs to be placed at doorways and windows for protection. Fennel, if collected at Midsummer's Eve, can be hung over the entrance doors. And you might consider using a bunch of fennel to splash salt water around the house or to sprinkle the water around each door and window. Other herbs, such as camphor or caraway, could also be used in the water.

St. John's Wort is a particularly effective protective herb. Because it corresponds with the fire element, you can burn St. John's Wort in the hearth of the house or, if you have no hearth, try burning it in a cauldron placed as close to the heart of your home as possible. To ensure that the magic continues in the form of good fortune, you could also plant basil or dill in a window box or herb garden, or plant a tree, such as the rowan or mountain ash, to watch over your house and family.

Doing a House Blessing or Cleansing

An effective house blessing or cleansing is to walk slowly around the outside of the house splashing water into which salt or any other herb you may wish to use has been added. As in Circle work, walk around the house deosil, clockwise. Keeping the clockwise motion, enter the house and, taking a candle, light it at the entrance. The sign of the pentagram with your athame or knife should be made at the entrance door as a protective symbol.

Move through the house, room to room, concentrating on the candle you are carrying while keeping an eye on where you are going. In each room make the sign of the pentagram at the door and at all windows. If appropriate, take a basket with you that contains the protective amulets prepared by you, and place one above each door and window.

Protecting Your House

Herbs are an effective way of protecting your house (*see* table on page 85), but there are other simple magical spells that can be worked. If you you are an embroiderer or sew your own clothes, you may consider the following charm to protect your house.

Keep a small jar beside you whenever you sew and each time you finish with a piece of thread and there is a little left over, pop it into the jar and say the words "protect this house from hardship and harm". Eventually, the jar will fill up and it can be sealed with a protective herb, such as St. John's Wort or a bay leaf, placed just under the lid. You can then store the jar in the highest place in the house, such as the attic or hung from the rafters.

THE MAGIC OF NATURE

Stone Magic

To use the magic of precious and semi-precious stones, it is important to gather over a period of time the stones that speak to you about certain issues in your life. The process involves keeping a conscious thought in your mind about a certain issue, say financial gain, before you choose a stone. For some people, the first stone they put their hands on while focusing on the desired outcome becomes the stone that will represent that issue for them. Others will need to handle a number of stones before feeling certain that the stone they are holding is the one relevant to the issue. With this latter technique, there is scope for finding several stones that represent shades of the issue, such as financial gain through your own efforts by finding a better paid job or through an unforeseen circumstance or windfall.

As you collect your stones, cleanse them with salt water or in a natural stream to remove any previous negative vibrations, then store them in a special box or basket, preferably lined with natural fabric, such as cotton or silk, to keep them safe. Include in your box a list of your stones and their correlations with specific circumstances, for example, a piece of rose quartz and love.

The stones can be used in your sacred space in conjunction with the elements. If you need to clear your mind about a certain issue represented by the stone, work with the air element and perhaps think of a spell that you can repeat with the stone in your hand. If you wish to strengthen your will for a particular purpose, use the element of fire by activating the energy of the stone near a candle flame and imagining the success of your wish as you stare into the flame. If you need to work with your emotions, wash your stone with water, and if you need to change your lifestyle in relation to your stone's issue, try combining your stone with the appropriate herb (*see* table on page 85). Some stones are naturally charged by particular herbs, for instance topaz and chalcedony are magically charged by peppermint.

Stone Magic for Healing

Semi-precious stones and gems can also be used for healing purposes. It has been suggested that the color of the stone can help ascertain the type of healing for which that stone can be used.

The most basic colors are the colors of the rainbow which are linked to the seven chakras or energy centers running along the human trunk and head. Any stone tending toward red, such as red jasper, will strengthen your health, while blue stones, such as lapis lazuli, tend to have a calming effect. Stones of the color green, such as moss agate or bloodstone, are thought to be general healers, and should be used when in doubt or as a general tonic.

TABLE OF STONES AND GEMS FOR PARTICULAR MAGICAL PURPOSES AND HEALING

Stone	Magical Properties	Healing Properties
Agate	improves energy	vision
Amethyst	aids meditation, dream magic	nerves
Bloodstone	relieves depression	hemorrhages
Diamond	strengthens incantations	lymph system, insomnia
Emerald	aids prophesy	general healing
Garnet	heightens sexuality	anemia
Jade	aids discovery of beauty	kidney and stomach
Lapis Lazuli	gives spiritual strength	rheumatism
Opal	accesses spirit world	heart
Pearl	releases anger	nerves
Turquoise	acts as a good luck charm	eyes

Flower Magic

Peony

Flower magic is a very sensitive and delicate art that uses cut flowers. The life span of cut flowers is short, and it is believed that the spirit of the flower dies with the flower, so the use of dried petals is discouraged. Like stone magic, flower magic is a tool that is developed according to your own reactions to the flower, your readings about its properties and times of flowering. You must also become familiar with the smell of the flower and study how it affects you. It is a very personal magic with emphasis on the flower's scent and color.

Certain flowers are also herbs. However, for flower magic purposes they are used in a way different from herbs — their magic is utilized mainly through their scent. Flower magic can be practiced in your own sacred space or you could keep the flower near you by your bed and ask that the answer you seek to your question comes to you in your dreams.

How to Use Flower Magic

You may wish to choose a particular element to work with your flower. If you work with the air element, you may burn the flower's essential oil and concentrate on the vapors rising from your oil burner. As you focus on the vapor, watching its twists and turns, see if it begins to form shapes or suggest ideas to you that provide an answer to your problem. If you use the fire element, rub the oil of the flower on the candle or make a candle that includes the flower's essential oil in its wax — you may decorate the base or length of the candle with the flower head. Once the candle burns down, your wish or the answer that you seek will start coming to you. Should you choose the water element, place an unopened bud of your flower in a glass or a bowl of water during the full moon. When the flower blooms, your wish will start to blossom as well.

If the earth element appeals to you, try creating a magical garden, planting the seeds of your favorite flowers charged with a purpose you wish to see fulfilled. Planting such a garden will give you a further appreciation of the flowers with which you feel attuned. You will become aware of when the seeds need to be planted, what soil is required and the best companion plants for a healthy garden grown without the need for pesticides. Tending a garden such as this will provide a powerful bonding with the flowers you wish to use for your magic.

TABLE OF FLOWERS

Flowers	Properties
Cornflower	abundance, fertility
Daisy	clarity, playfulness in times of stress
Jasmine	sensual love
Lavender	unresolved guilt
Peony	protection from negative energy
Rose (red)	love, passion
Sunflower	strength, courage, the balancing of self-esteem
Tulip	the mending of bonds
Violets	comfort in times of sorrow
Water lily	love, calm
White lily	spirituality, an open heart
Wisteria	stimulation of the brain for study

DIVINATION

Reading Tea Leaves

Tea leaf reading, otherwise known as tasseography, is a form of divination that works on the shapes that the tea leaves form and the closeness of the leaves to the rim of the cup. It is believed that China tea provides the best results.

The person for whom you are doing the divination must first drink the tea. Once the tea is drunk and only a small amount of liquid is left, ask your friend to rotate the cup three times clockwise and then turn the cup over onto the saucer. The excess water drains away and the leaves that are left in the cup are distributed to the cup's rim. The immediate future can be read from the tea leaves gathered closest to the rim. Look further into the cup to read events in the distant future.

TABLE OF TEA LEAF SYMBOLS

Shape	Meaning
Bell	wedding
Butterfly	insincerity
Cat	domestic problems
Cross	hardship
Cup	harmony
Dog	friendship
Hand	help
Heart	love
House	security
Key	opportunity
Tree	comfort
Snake	hurt feelings

You will be looking for the shapes that the tea leaves make. You may see an anchor, an equal-armed cross or the shape of a house, among many other possibilities. Each shape has its own interpretation. As always with divination skills, it is also important to acknowledge *how you feel* about the symbol and its meaning for your friend. That always overrides set interpretations. It is believed that if the shapes are clear, luck is on your friend's side, and if they are hazy, your friend's future is much more prone to hindrances and unexpected delays.

Crystal Scrying

Scrying is a means of divination that interprets pictures, both moving or static, that appear to form through a mist in a crystal ball or in the smoke swirling inside a cauldron. Crystal scrying requires a flawless crystal ball that can ideally be placed on a black velvet cloth. Perspex colorless balls may also be used as a cheaper alternative, but must be kept carefully to avoid any scratches. It is recommended that you practice your scrying within your sacred place, preferably at night and in quiet. This form of divination requires concentration, so you may wish to use an incense designed to help you focus, such as myrrh or even peppermint. You may also need to practice for at least a week before you begin to see anything in the ball.

How to Read a Crystal Ball

The first step is to sit in front of the ball and keep your mind blank. Gaze, but do not stare, into the crystal. Eventually it will appear to be filling with a slight mist. The mist should become denser until it clears, revealing a picture. Your next step will be to interpret the pictures you see. You may seek enlightenment from set dream symbols or from your own dream journal, as well as any other associations that come to mind.

THE WIZARD'S WORLD

CEREMONIAL MAGICIAN OR SATANIST?

In this book, we have divided the different approaches to magic between the kitchen witch and the ceremonial magician or wizard. Historically, the word "magician" is more or less interchangeable with wizard. In Chapter 4, The Witch's World, we looked at magical practices and divination techniques that use natural objects and rely on intuition and other right-brain functions. Here, we look at magic that has evolved into systems of occult logic and at occult institutions which are hierarchical and were initially male dominated. The ritual of Drawing down the Sun is practiced by males, while working with a particular god is appropriate for both genders. The analytical functions of the left brain predominates much of the wizard's magic.

Ceremonial magic uses elaborate ritual from a sophisticated occult system. Many of these have roots in the Middle East, deriving from Egyptian, Islamic and Jewish traditions. The arts of mathematics, astrology, alchemy and ritual magic proliferated in these regions and were exported westward by Crusaders in the twelfth century and, in later years, through Moorish and Jewish expansion. In the late-nineteenth century, interest in these systems again emerged and blossomed (see "Aleister Crowley" on page 31 and "Hermetic Order of the Golden Dawn" on page 34).

Modern witches and wizards who practice white magic do not worship Satan or the Devil. Some Satanic orders do exist but they constitute a minor part of the occult community. The concept of good and evil as the two major poles of energy are not a concept used in modern witchcraft. The polarity is between male and female. In most Wiccan traditions, the masculine energy of the cosmos is worshiped equally with the feminine energy. This male energy becomes personified as the consort of the goddess, aiding her in her role as earth mother. He is known by many names, such as the Lord, Herne the Hunter, Cernunnos, Odin, Osiris and, of course, the "Great God Pan".

An astrological map from the Sea Atlas, c.1800, by Johannes Van Keulen.

POPULAR PAGAN GODS

The Lord

In Wicca, the Lord is consort to the Lady and is the essence of masculine energy. He is the Lady's lover and son, his role personifying the progress of the seasons through the year. He takes on three major functions during the cycle of the seasons that reflect the three aspects of the goddess, as Maid, Mother and Crone. However, his path is slightly different to that of the goddess. He creates, dies and is then reborn. In the beginning of the cycle, he is lover to the goddess as the maiden.

As a fertility god or Lord of Creation, he is known, in Celtic mythology, as Pan, Cernunnos or Herne the Hunter. When he gives his seed to the goddess, he slowly dies and becomes Lord of the Underworld, reflecting the crone aspect of the goddess. In this phase, he is known as Osiris in Egyptian mythology. At Yule, or "Christmas" time, his seed comes to fruition and the goddess gives him rebirth. In this phase he was, in certain cultures, known as the Sun god – born on the longest, darkest night of the year. It was believed that with his re/birth the darkness of the season ended. This was strengthened by the fact that from the winter solstice (Yule) the days started to get longer.

He is also known as Lord of the Dance. This title encompasses all his roles as consort to the Lady. The "dance" is a reference to the dance of life – of creation, death and rebirth. In Celtic mythology, the Lord rides on a wild hunt. At Samhain, or Halloween (All Hallow's Eve) he becomes Lord of the Underworld, riding with a pack of restless dead, searching for souls. To Wiccans, he is both wild and wise.

The Horned God

The Horned God, Herne the Hunter, Pan and Cernunnos are all names of gods who have a number of similarities. All are deities linked with powerful animal images, such as the stag which, in turn, is symbolic of fertility. Its antlers are a sign of virility as well as being symbolic of the crescent moon.

The Horned God is also known as Lord of the Forest and as consort to the goddess is one of the most popular images in modern witchcraft. He is the god of sexuality, the underworld and animals and, like the Greek god Pan, is depicted as half man, half animal, an image taken in Christianity to represent the Devil. He is often referred to as Cernunnos by modern witches and wizards – a Celtic god of the hunt and fertility.

Herne the Hunter is believed to be the underworld aspect of the Horned God and, as such, leads a pack of spectral huntsmen at Samhain. He is associated with the oak, and there is a belief that he appears in Windsor Forest in Britain when the nation is in jeopardy. Pan, a Greek god, is better known for his virility and attendant nymphs, and is invoked for his playful sexuality.

Pan and Psyche *by Sir Edward Burne-Jones (1833 – 98).*

Odin

The leader of the Norse and Germanic pantheon, Odin or Wotan is the true magician's deity. He had a huge appetite for forbidden knowledge and was accredited as being a powerful magician and healer. His quest for knowledge leads him to wander the earth in a long dark cloak and a large hat which hides the loss of one eye. The eye was sacrificed for a drink from a spring flowing under the roots of the Nordic great world tree — Yggdrasil.

The waters contained wisdom and discernment. As he imbibed, he found that he was thirsty for even more knowledge. Odin chose to hang from Yggdrasil without food and water and with a

spear in his side for nine days. It was while he was in a trance hanging from Yggdrasil that Odin was able to learn the magic of the runes, which would be used later as an alphabet for learning and utilized for magical purposes, such as amulets.

It is thought that Odin may have been a real person whose myth grew over the passage of time. He was certainly not entirely benevolent, as he had a reputation for being manipulative and a shapeshifter at whim. (A shapeshifter is someone who is able to change his or her shape at will to that of his or her animal spirit.) Consequently, Odin was also renowned for his shamanistic abilities and astral travels, riding to visit the various worlds of Norse mythology on his eight-legged horse, Sleipnir, to gather even more information and knowledge.

Osiris

Osiris is the Lord of the Dead in Egyptian mythology and was brother and husband to the goddess Isis (*see* Chapter 4, page 76). Originally worshiped as the spirit of the River Nile, he would rise annually to fertilize the land, symbolized by Isis. With the evolution of the Egyptian pantheon, Osiris and Isis became the great-grandchildren of the sun god Ra and went on to become king and queen of Egypt. Osiris's legendary reign, not unlike that of King Arthur in Britain, symbolized a golden age of peace and civilization in Egypt. Agricultural development and religious stability were important cornerstones of his reign.

Osiris ruled for 28 years until his brother Set murdered him and cut his body into 14 pieces. Isis was responsible for finding most of the pieces and magically transforming him whole and making him immortal. At this point Osiris chose to become Lord of the Dead. They coupled one more time and a son was born. He was named Horus, and Horus was to avenge his father's death and came to be known as Lord of the Living. Osiris cared for and judged the dead and granted immortality to the deserving, and Set, who represented the desert, was banished from the valley.

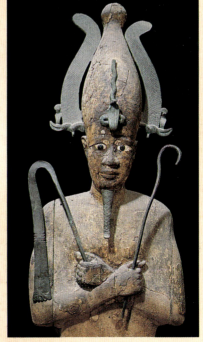

Opposite: Odin is traditionally depicted as a wanderer, constantly questing for knowledge.

Right: Osiris was the Egyptian god of vegetation and resurrection.

INVOKING THE GOD

Drawing down the Sun

In Chapter 4 we discussed Drawing down the Moon, where the high priestess of a Circle becomes the channel for the goddess (*see* page 80). There is a similar ritual in some traditions for the high priest of a Circle to become the channel for the god. The ritual, called Drawing down the Sun, is not used so often in Wiccan circles but its relevance is beginning to grow. More and more men are trying to recapture their innate masculine energy, which provides insight into a more compassionate and sensual way of being, moving away from society's preconceptions of men as either aggressive, testosterone-laden he-men or sensitive New Age wimps.

The Ritual

For a wizard working solitary, Drawing down the Sun can be done in your sacred space by imagining that you can feel the warming rays of the sun upon you. You may also wish to time your working when the sun's rays pass over your sacred space. Feel the rays penetrating your skin, charging your nerve endings. Imagine the energy in your nerve endings running toward the core of your body, lighting up the seven chakras along your spine — first at the base of your spine, then between the pubic bone and your belly button, your solar plexus, your heart, your throat, in the middle of your forehead and, finally, at the crown of your head. Feel the energy of the sun cleansing you and clearing any blockages you may have.

Working with a Particular God — a Formal Ritual

If you are working within a Circle with another person or a group, you may wish to work with a particular god for a certain festival, celebrating the Wheel of the Year. Choose the god well and make sure it is a suitable time of the year for him to be invoked. There is a tradition in Celtic witchcraft that you do not choose a god, he chooses you (*see* Chapter 1, page 12).

One technique is to allow yourself to be open to the masculine energy and see which god form appears to you. To do this, perhaps in a group working, you may wish to Draw down the Sun. This working comes straight after Drawing down the Moon. It is not the usual practice of many Wiccans to Draw down the Sun; however, where the high priest feels that he needs to link into the masculine energy for the purpose of the working, it is a useful ritual to perform. The high priest faces his high priestess and she, already channeling the goddess, will invoke the god into him by words or a gesture. Although it is not usual practice, it may be appropriate that the high priest will need to give a charge of the god, which will bring added meaning for the rest of the group as to the purpose of the Circle.

The Sun Rises While the Moon Sleeps, *1990, by Peter Davidson (living artist).*

MALE MYSTERIES

Druids

The Druids were Celtic priests whose rituals and knowledge were largely kept secret. Their traditions were not written down, and it is open to speculation exactly what the Druids did from the fifth century B.C. until their suppression by the Romans in the first century A.D. Their skills included herbalism, divination, astronomy, poetry, and interpreting omens that occurred in nature, such as the flight of certain birds. Their beliefs included reincarnation and the power of the earth. The eight seasonal festivals in the Wheel of the Year were also celebrated by the Druids. The depth of their interest and understanding of the natural world was their strength. The term Druid is a Gaelic word meaning "knowledge of the oak tree". Oak leaves were often used in Druidic ceremonies, and rituals were thought to have been held in sacred oak groves.

One of the main reasons given by the Romans for their suppression of the Druids was their practice of ritually burning alive both animal and human sacrifices in wicker cages. It was by watching the death throes of the sacrifices that the Druids were able to do a rather grisly form of divinatory work. They were also expert at interpreting dreams and making charms.

The Druids fell into decline when many of them were killed by the Romans. However, a romanticized version of the Druids was revived in the sixteenth and seventeenth centuries. It was during this time the now discredited theory emerged that the Druids built Stonehenge. By the end of the eighteenth century, the Ancient Order of Druids was established.

*Druids Sacrificing to the Sun in their Temple called Stonehenge, engraved by
Nathaniel Whittock (1791 – 1860) from a plan of Stonehenge by Dr Stukeley in the
Ashmolean Museum, Oxford.*

Rosicrucians

In the late nineteenth century, a Rosicrucian Society was founded, which was also known as the *Societas Rosicruciana in Anglia*. Rosicrucianism was said to have been developed as a secret Fraternity of the Rosy Cross by a mythical character called Christian Rosenkreutz (Christian Rosycross) in fifteenth-century Germany. Members of the Fraternity were believed to possess magical powers and were encouraged to develop their spirituality by advancement through a number of grades and rituals. To become a Rosicrucian in the nineteenth century, potential members had to first be members of the Freemasons. The Rosicrucians are said to have a stronger emphasis on the occult than the Freemasons and followed the principles evolved by Paracelsus in the sixteenth century (*see* Chapter 1, page 28).

Rosicrucians believe in reincarnation and clairvoyance, and one of their main symbols include a cross within a rose or a cross formed from the stem of a seven-petalled rose. This is believed to be a secret symbol, balancing the darkness of the cross with the spiritual enlightenment of the rose. The rose can also be interpreted as a symbol of secrecy and confidences being kept. The organization of the Rosicrucians was to prove a major influence on the structures of such occult organizations in the nineteenth century as the Hermetic Order of the Golden Dawn.

Freemasons

Freemasonry is a secret society open to men of good reputation. The society is divided into lodges, involving initiation into the society and progression through the different levels of the society, measured by degrees. Freemasonry accepts all forms of belief systems involving a supreme being, and many of its rituals are based on moral issues to do with charity, humanity and fraternity. This is also demonstrated outside the society where members of the Freemasons are known to help each other in material matters. The society developed as a type of network for masons working on large scale building projects. As masons were itinerant, it was important to implement a system in which masons working on new building sites were assured that they were working with masons of suitable experience and character. Lodges were often set up at major building sites and a mason would be interviewed to make sure that he was a Master Mason. Secret handshakes, passwords and signs were used to ascertain whether someone had previously been a member of a Lodge at another building site.

A splinter group, called the Co-Masons, continued the same structure as the Freemasons but allowed women as members. This group was founded in 1902.

Masonic Regalia from the Order of Turin.

ANCIENT MYSTERIES

Kabbala

The kabbala is an ancient Hebrew system of magic that has had a profound effect on the work of the wizard. The kabbala, also known as cabala or qabalah, uses the symbol of the Tree of Life, which defines ten levels or sephiroth of consciousness or energies between humankind and the spiritual higher being which is called, in the Kabbalistic tradition, *Ain Soph*. The original Jewish version of the kabbala envisioned a monotheistic version with only one god in its various aspects. However, in other systems of magic, the kabbala has been adapted to reflect a polytheistic system.

The wizard attempts to work his way up the paths to the various energy levels, starting at Malkuth, which symbolizes earthly preoccupations, and then moves up the following nine levels, which can be equated with the potential of humankind:

Yesod – the Foundation, representing sexual drives.

Hod – Splendor, representing the intellect and reason.

Netzach – Victory, representing love and the emotions.

Tiphareth – Beauty, Harmony, representing the Messiah.

Geburah – Severity, Strength, War, representing the warring god.

Chesed – Mercy, Peace, Order, representing the compassionate god.

Binah – Understanding, representing the Great Mother.

Chokmah – Wisdom, representing the Great Father.

Kether – the Crown of Creation, representing infinite bliss.

There are thirty-two paths (including the sephrioth themselves) that the wizard can follow to attain his own revelations concerning his psyche. The kabbala recognizes that the ten levels are equally holy and, by learning the correspondences between the levels and objects of the real world, the adept may cast spells. Correspondences are, for example, colors, herbs, oils, planets or trees that have a specific magical vibration that can be used in conjunction with the appropriate spell or working. All the tables given in this book are essentially correspondences.

Connections not used by classical kabbalists have evolved, the Tree of Life being a very useful framework to understand Western symbols and philosophies. In the late nineteenth century, a connection was made between paths linking the ten levels and the Major Arcana of the Tarot.

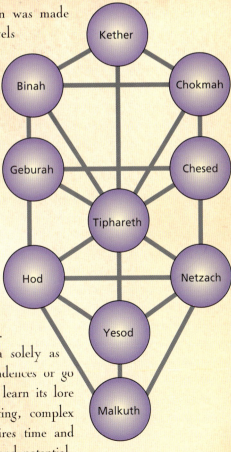

One of the aims of many occult philosophies is to link into the energy of the gods. The level of Tiphareth is midway between the Infinite of the higher spiritual being and the Finite of earth. The level symbolizes harmony and was thought to be the highest level of experience to which members of the Hermetic Order of the Golden Dawn (*see* Chapter 1, page 34) aspired.

Wizards can use the kabbala solely as framework for magical correspondences or go back to the original system and learn its lore and symbolism. It is a fascinating, complex and profound system that requires time and study to understand its nuances and potential.

Grimoires

Grimoires are books of magic, containing spells, incantations, correspondences and ritual practices that were used by wizards since the thirteenth century. Much of their content was said to have been derived from ancient magical texts. Originally copied by hand, with the advent of the printing press in the late fifteenth century, a number of printed grimoires came into circulation, their popularity peaking in the late nineteenth century.

Grimoires originally were used by wizards for black magic purposes to conjure and use demons to obtain power and wealth. How to conjure particular demons by the right incantation, incense and prayer, and information about precisely what time the demon could be conjured, were all outlined in the grimoire.

The most important grimoire is *The Key of Solomon,* which was thought to have been written by the legendary King Solomon and has been the basis of many later grimoires, such as *The Secrets of Secrets,* otherwise known as *True Black Magic,* which was written in the eighteenth century. The origin of *The Key of Solomon* is difficult to pinpoint as there have been many versions of it through the centuries. A Greek version, dating between 1,100–1,200 A.D., is in the British Museum. Another grimoire attributed to King Solomon is called *The Lesser Key of Solomon* which includes information suitable for white magic.

The Key of Solomon contains many spells and charms, including a spell for flying. The spell can only be performed on one day of the year — June 25 — and involves the skin of a stag and the blood of a hare, a rod made from oak, a sprig of mugwort, and the eyes of a particular fish. To fly, the wizard puts on two garters made from the stag's skin and which are filled with mugwort and fish eyes. He then must write his destination on the ground using the oak rod, whilst facing in the right direction. Apparently, the garters will fly at once.

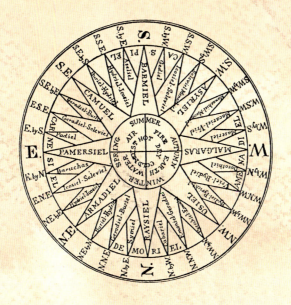

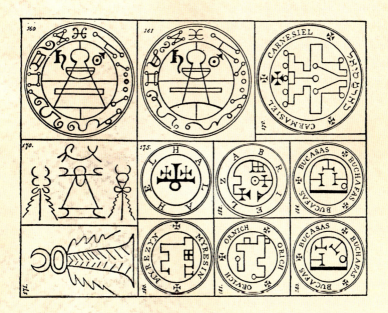

The symbols from The Lesser Key of King Solomon are referred to in white magic.

DIVINATION

Astrology

Astrology is one of the oldest and most popular forms of divination. Believed to be one of humankind's earliest magical practices, astrology is the observation of the sun, moon and heavenly bodies and how their movements appear to correspond to various aspects of human life.

The process of astrology relates to the concept that whatever is happening in the cosmos is reflected in the physical world. The concept that "as above, so below" is an important one, derived from the Hermetic belief system, as discussed in the Hermetic Order of the Golden Dawn in Chapter 1, page 34.

Astrology is a precise system that requires study and contemplation before it can be fully mastered. As a system, it is thought to have been developed around 3,000 B.C. The idea that there were 12 constellations through which the sun, moon and planets traveled was developed early, and over the centuries astrologers began to see the correlation between a person's fate and the position of the heavenly bodies at his or her birth. The Greeks, the Chinese, the Hindus and the Tibetans all developed their own form of astrology. Historically, astrology, which was once studied along with alchemy and medicine, lost popularity through the eighteenth century — the Age of Reason — when it was decried as a "disgrace to Reason".

However, as natural magic continued to be practiced, the correspondence between the cosmic movements of the sun, moon and planets, and the elements, herbs, stones and the timing of certain rituals again became a popular study. Wizards noticed

This stained-glass window depicts the signs of the zodiac, with the sun and moon at its center.

that the observance of astrological principles added power to their rituals. Wizards were also approached to prepare horoscopes for people and to divine when important events would happen. Dr. John Dee was employed by Elizabeth, the imprisoned half-sister of Queen Mary, to find out when Mary would die, so that she could set an auspicious date for her coronation.

TABLE OF ASTROLOGICAL CORRESPONDENCES

Star signs	Planets	Elements	Herbs
Aries	Mars	Fire	Chili, marjoram
Taurus	Venus	Earth	Cumin, lovage
Gemini	Mercury	Air	Meadowsweet
Cancer	Moon	Water	Honeysuckle
Leo	Sun	fire	St. John's Wort
Virgo	Mercury	Earth	Lavender
Libra	Venus	Air	Rose geranium
Scorpio	Mars	Water	Basil
Sagittarius	Jupiter	Fire	Dandelion
Capricorn	Saturn	Earth	Comfrey
Aquarius	Uranus	Air	Star anise
Pisces	Neptune	Water	Hemp

Numerology

Bust of Pythagoras,
c. 582 – 497 B.C.

Divination using numerology is related to astrology. There are a number of systems that evolved from the wisdom of Pythagoras, a sixth-century B.C. Greek philosopher, who believed that the world was built upon the power of numbers. It is believed that names, house numbers and birth dates can, when reduced to a single digit, reveal many hidden qualities. The numbers one to nine were assigned by Pythagoras and others with certain qualities. It was thought that even numbers, such as 2, 4, 6 and 8 represented stability, while odd numbers represented creativity.

To ascertain your Birth number, add up all the digits of your birth date, then add the two digits of the total to arrive at a single number, unless your number adds up to 11, 22 or 33. These three numbers are thought to be "master numbers" and are symbolic of a path aligned with higher spirituality.

For instance, 29 March 1963
$$= 2 + 9 + 3 + 1 + 9 + 6 + 3$$
$$= 33$$

To ascertain your Name number, assign a number for each letter in your name using the following table:

1	2	3	4	5	6	7	8	9
A	B	C	D	E	F	G	H	I
J	K	L	M	N	O	P	Q	R
S	T	U	V	W	X	Y	Z	

For instance, Mina Adams
$$= 4 + 9 + 5 + 1 + 1 + 4 + 1 + 4 + 1$$
$$= 30$$
$$= 3$$

The kabbalists were very taken by numerology and used numbers in magical squares to create powerful amulets and talismans. There is magic in a square of numbers in which the numbers are so arranged that no matter how they are added up, either horizontally or vertically, the answer is the same. The kabbalists devised seven magical squares that were linked to five planets visible to the naked eye as well as the sun and moon. These were thought to be so powerful that the demons associated with each square could be called to do the summoner's bidding.

TABLE OF MEANING IN NUMEROLOGY

Number	Meaning
1	Ambitious, commanding, extrovert, strong
2	Introvert, sensitive, emotional, imaginative
3	Seeks knowledge, humorous, dedicated, trusting
4	Intuitive, interest in spirituality, seeks justice
5	Friendly, active, orderly, methodical
6	Pleasant, peaceful, friendly, refined
7	Introvert, psychic, interest in the cosmos
8	Successful, materialistic, seeks justice
9	Emotional, jealous, active, loyal, impulsive

Tarot

The Tarot deck is a form of divination that is thought to have evolved from ancient Egyptian magical texts. Historically, however, there are no records of the Tarot until the fourteenth century. The Tarot is a deck of 78 cards, which is divided into the Major Arcana of 22 cards and the Minor Arcana of 56 cards. The Minor Arcana is divided into four groups, representing the four elements. Each group of the Minor Arcana concerns a certain aspect of life, for instance:

TABLE OF MEANINGS – THE MINOR ARCANA

Minor Arcana Suit	Symbol in Modern Playing Cards	Aspect
Wands	Clubs	Enterprise and imagination
Cups	Hearts	Love and happiness
Pentacles	Diamonds	Money
Swords	Spades	Obstacles or matters of the intellect

Each of the Minor Arcana suites has four court cards and ten numbered cards. The court cards – the King, Queen, Knight and Page – usually represent people: a dominant male or male characteristic; a dominant female; an ambitious person; and a youngster. In the numbered cards, there is also a consistent interpretation of numbers across the four suits, such as:

TABLE OF MEANINGS – THE NUMBERED CARDS

Number	Meaning
Ace	New beginnings
2	Balance required
3	Growth
4	Stability
5	Change, uncertainty
6	Harmony
7	Endings
8	Balance achieved
9	Achievement
10	Completion

The Major Arcana represents 22 aspects of the human life and can be summarized in the following table:

TABLE OF MEANINGS – THE MAJOR ARCANA

Card Number	Name	Meaning
0	The Fool	Setting out on a journey
1	The Magician	Powerful guidance
2	The High Priestess	Spiritual knowledge
3	The Empress	Growth
4	The Emperor	Responsibility
5	The High Priest	Spiritual wisdom
6	The Lovers	Choice
7	The Chariot	Direction in life
8	Justice	Weighing up the pros and cons
9	The Hermit	Withdrawal
10	The Wheel of Fortune	Randomness
11	Strength	Determination
12	The Hanged Man	Self-sacrifice
13	Death	Transition
14	Temperance	Harmony and healing
15	The Devil	Pride and arrogance
16	The Tower	Upheaval
17	The Star	Hope
18	The Moon	Absence of reason
19	The Sun	Fulfillment
20	Judgement	Readiness for rebirth
21	The World	Success

To use the Tarot, keep a question in mind, and shuffle the cards. Many patterns can be adopted to help read the solution. The Celtic Cross pattern is particularly good for understanding what issues you have been dealing with in the past and what will come up in the future before your issue can be resolved. Experiment with some of the many Tarot decks now available, finding the images that help you link into your intuition.

THE PATH OF MAGIC

RITUAL OBSERVANCE OF NATURE

There are two types of rituals that witches and wizards tend to observe during a year. The first and most important group of rituals celebrate the Wheel of the Year, the progress of the seasons with the god in his aspects as Lord of Creation, Lord of the Underworld and the Son Reborn.

There are eight sabbats, four major and four lesser, that relate to the solstices and equinoxes, all of which mark the changes in the seasons. These are rituals that mark the passage of the Sun through the Heavens and its effects on earth. Sabbat rituals are a way of tuning into the earth's energy and aligning one's purpose and life to the mood of the earth. Spells may be worked at these times, if their importance warrants it; for instance, if there is the need for a particularly powerful healing, perhaps for an individual who is seriously ill, or if energy is being directed to a group that is doing something useful for the world and needs help, Amnesty International being a good example. Strong, extroverted techniques, such as chanting, ecstatic dancing and sex magic, are often practiced during these rituals. Many witches and wizards will, however, treat sabbats as purely celebratory and devotional occasions.

The second type of ritual, called Esbats, concerns the passage of the moon through her phases where the goddess is seen in her aspects as Maid, Mother and Crone. Moon rituals are an excellent time to cast healing, love and money spells, to make charms, and to use trance work and meditation to aid the solution of a problem. These are gentler rituals that use techniques much more introspective than those used for the sabbats.

Phases of the Moon

Traditionally it was thought that occult power was at its height at full moon, but each aspect of the goddess as waxing and waning moon has its own power that can be tapped by a witch or wizard. The goddess, through the moon, rules the oceans and the seas. She is the ebb and flow of creation and death. As a witch or wizard, to truly understand the goddess and the moon, you must live your life according to all her phases.

Look at what is happening in your everyday life and see if there are correspondences with the moon's phase. Many ordinary desk diaries have the phases of the moon noted. If you keep a diary or journal, check the previous dates and notice whether you were, for instance, able to finish a project near waxing moon. Becoming aware of how the earth's energies work gives you enormous power, because you are then able to work with these energies to achieve your own projects and ambitions rather than relying solely on your own energy.

Another way to link into the phases of the moon and what they mean to you is to set time aside to meditate on the three aspects of the goddess. You can do this in your own sacred space. Set aside one night for each aspect, ideally the night of the appropriate phase of the moon. For each phase, if you can see the moon, focus on it and imagine the Maid, Mother and Crone as yourself. Initiate a conversation with this other self and listen to her wisdom. Become familiar with her because, once established, you may seek her advice and guidance about a particular issue.

OBSERVING THE SEASONS

The eight festivals occur approximately every six weeks throughout the year. A sabbat is the high point of a seasonal phase, which is celebrated by banquets and rituals to underline its significance and importance of the season. However, it is equally important to observe all the everyday activities and changes in energy flows that precede a new festival. As with the observance of the moon, keep a journal that shows your everyday activities and the success or otherwise of your projects. Have you ever noticed that money or recognition always happens at around harvest time if you have planned wisely?

The Chinese were well aware of the effects of the changes of season and their influence on their health. With each season, the Chinese would eat different foods prepared in different ways. For instance, for summer, light vegetables with a high moisture content would be eaten, cooked quickly in the wok. During winter, root vegetables were eaten more and longer cooking processes were used, such as baking. The food you prepare for festivals can also embody this wisdom — an excellent way of strongly linking into the mood of the sabbat through the produce of the earth. In an age when fruits and vegetables can be grown all year round in greenhouses, try to vary your diet to suit when the fruits and vegetables are naturally in season.

By flowing with the energy of the season you will be surprised how much your energy increases, because you are not acting against nature's wisdom. Similarly, the Chinese believed that during winter, as the earth sleeps so should human beings rest more. During this time the body should be given a chance to recharge, to get itself ready for the challenge of spring and the high energy needed to get through summer.

*A beech tree forest in Buckinghamshire, England, displays
the colors of autumn, one of the most beautiful seasonal changes in nature.*

UNDERSTANDING THE FORCES OF NATURE

Since ancient times, witches and wizards have been accredited with the knowledge of how to change the weather and raise storms. In medieval times, knotted ropes were sold to seamen in the belief that each knot contained the power to raise winds. If a little bit of breeze was needed to stir the sails, the seaman would unknot only one knot, if a good healthy gust was required, he would unknot a few more knots.

Witchcraft relies on the understanding of the elements. In time, legend came to state that, through so close an association, witches and wizards were empowered to cause all manner of tempests, storms and strong destructive winds. Originally, Egyptian magicians were called upon to raise gales to halt enemy marauders but, with the Magical Art's gradual fall from grace, by the Middle Ages natural disasters were almost always seen to be the fault of a witch or wizard. The spells for the control of the elements were always highly unpleasant, usually involving the sacrifice of a living creature, such as a cockerel in a cauldron or a bucket of urine that would be transformed into rain.

In modern witchcraft, a spell to bind an enemy through the control of the weather is not encouraged unless under the direct circumstances. However, rituals can be devised that focus on ending a drought or stemming the overflow of a river.

Spring Tide near Honfleur, c.1861, by Paul Huet (1803 – 69).

MOON RITUALS AND PRACTICES

Full Moon

Full moon is the time for most workings that involve healing, divination and the making of amulets and talismans for a specific purpose such as emotional protection of yourself or others. It is thought that the fullness of the moon relates to a heightened level of spiritual energy that can be used for white magic. Spells are also made at this time in relation to the protection of the house or to help find a new home.

Ritual

Feminine energy is high during the full moon and echoes the maturity of the goddess as the earth mother. This is the ideal time to work with her energy to balance any sense of inadequacy in yourself. Once you have set up your sacred space, created your Circle and invited the elements and the Lord and the Lady, draw down the energy of the Lady. Imagine her as a warm and caring person who loves you without reservation. Imagine a sense of warmth and nurturance as you feel the Lady embrace you with affection. Feel her support travel through your body to your spine, which will straighten with a feeling of strength and confidence.

To heighten the vibration of the Circle you may wish to decorate your space with herbs and flowers relevant to the moon, such as jasmine, lily and the white rose. If you partake of wine and cakes, which is the symbolic partaking of the bounty of the Lord and Lady, you may wish to bake circular cookies for full moon and crescent-shaped cookies for new moon rituals.

New Moon

A new moon ritual is a perfect time to seek aid and guidance about a project, relationship or career. The time of the new moon is that of the wild and undirected energies of the goddess as the maid and virgin. Her energies are young and strong. This is the time when ideas abound, some fantastic and some bright and ambitious. Knowing which ideas to pursue can sometimes be difficult, so you may seek guidance from the new energy of the moon and, always a good idea, a blessing for its outcome.

Night, by Giuseppe Bonito (1707 – 89).

Ritual

There are many ways you can celebrate a new moon ritual. As always set up your Circle space, draw your circle and invite the elements and the Lord and the Lady in her guise as the maid. It is suggested that, when you draw down the Lady's energy into yourself, imagine her as Diana the huntress whose aim is straight and accurate. Use this energy to feel Diana showing you what preparations you need to make so that your aim with your project is as accurate as Diana is with her arrows. You may wish to focus this energy into a young plant that you have brought into Circle with you, preferably one that grows straight up, and keep it as a reminder of your path. Each time you tend and water your plant, imagine your path growing stronger and the fulfillment of your project coming closer to fruition.

SEASONAL RITUALS AND PRACTICES

Know the Wheel of the Year

The Wheel of the Year refers to the eight seasonal sabbats that are celebrated by witches and wizards during the year. It concerns the passage of the sun through the heavens and focuses on the story of the god.

In midwinter, the goddess gives birth to a son who grows to adolescence by spring. In spring, the goddess appears to the god in a youthful form. She falls pregnant to him and grows in beauty as Mother of Life in summer and autumn. The god in the same time ages and dies slowly becoming the Lord of Death, symbolizing winter. In the darkest time, when the days are at their shortest, the goddess gives birth to the son, whom she will again take as a lover in spring, continuing the life cycle or spiral.

The sabbats are divided into two groups. The Greater Sabbats fall on dates that represent high energy in the season as shown in the table opposite.

The Lesser Sabbats fall on the equinoxes and solstices, the dates of which vary slightly from year to year. These sabbats, which mark the changes of the four seasons, are generally held according to the table opposite.

TABLE OF THE GREATER SABBATS

Wicca name	Other name	Northern Hemisphere Date	Southern Hemisphere Date
Samhain	Halloween	October 31	May 1
Imbolc	Candlemas	February 2	August 1
Beltane	May Day	May 1	October 31
Lammas	Lughnasadh	August 1	February 2

TABLE OF THE LESSER SABBATS

Wicca name	Other name	Northern Hemisphere Date (varies)	Southern Hemisphere Date (varies)
Yule	Midwinter Solstice	December 21–23	June 21–23
Ostara	Spring Equinox	March 21–23	September 21–23
Litha	Midsummer Solstice	June 21–23	December 21–23
Mabon	Autumn Equinox	September 21–23	March 21–23

During Samhain, the misty veils between the worlds may part, giving way to the new cycle.

Samhain (Halloween)

Celtic tradition begins the Wheel of the Year at Samhain, commencing a season of darkness where the veil between the worlds is thin. The god has descended into the underworld and a new god is growing within the goddess. This is the time when a small seed is shimmering in the depth of the earth, waiting to grow, and this is the time that a new cycle truly begins. It is a time of assessment, of making the final arrangements that will help the family survive the winter. In traditional villages, weak animals were slaughtered because they would not survive the harsh cold.

Ritual

Rituals around Samhain may be devised to help us understand and acknowledge our weaknesses, which we can write down on a piece of paper and ceremonially burn as a cleansing of the old. Samhain is an introspective time, we echo the descent of the god deep inside the earth, when work can be done to assess and retune ourselves and divest ourselves of traits that we no longer need.

It is a tradition at Yule to stay up all night, making sure the sun comes up in the morning.

Yule (Midwinter Solstice)

Other traditions start the Wheel of the Year at Yule, with the birth of the goddess's son. In the Christian calendar, Yule is known as Christmas. The Sun is at its lowest point in the heavens. The birth of new promise and hope is celebrated at this time, because from this day onward the nights will again become shorter and the days will be longer.

Ritual

Rituals around Yule can focus on what your new plans are going to be for the new year. Almost in the spirit of New Years' resolutions, you may wish to state some intentions. Wiccans believe that whatever you say as your intention must in fact be kept. Remember, it is one of the tenets of modern witchcraft that you must act according to your will. You may at this time receive some insight into what path you may take in the new year. This is seen by some as a gift from the god and the goddess. If you receive such a present, it would be appropriate to give something back to the earth during the following year.

Imbolc is a time of new beginnings, a reawakening.

Imbolc (Candlemas)

Imbolc is also known as Candlemas, a time of reawakening that is often accompanied by a mass of candles, lighting the way to new creativity, as the goddess, after giving birth to her son, is now emerging again as a young maid or the Virgin Queen. Her energy is wild and free, untamed and new. Imbolc celebrates the end of darkness and the reaffirmation of growth.

Ritual

Imbolc rituals can focus on awakening a sense of creativity within you — a creativity that may lead you into a deeper feeling of freedom. This is the time of inspiration and of initiation into a deeper sense of spirituality, opening the path to new experiences and an openness to learning new things. Rituals at this time can also focus on purification in the sense of the letting go of old bad habits and redundant aspects of our lives. The purification of sin is not a concept associated with witchcraft.

Ostara commences the current of spring and regrowth.

Ostara (Spring Equinox)

The first day of Spring is a time of a great sense of energy and promise. This is the time when the goddess is feeling and exploring her strength and beauty. However, she is not yet set on her path as mother of the god. This festival is equated with Easter in the Christian calendar. The same symbols for Easter, such as painted eggs, can be used in Ostara rituals.

Ritual

With the increase of the Sun's energy, the emphasis at Ostara is on fertility, in the sense of procreation and the increase in creative projects. The focus on birth and growth has been gathering momentum since Imbolc and rituals can focus on the maturing of your creative path chosen at Imbolc. This is a time for putting some energy back into the earth with rituals featuring the planting of flowers, trees and herbs with a blessing that dedicates each planting to the goddess in her aspect as Maiden.

Beltane (May Day)

At Beltane, the god and goddess have reached maturity and both consummate their love for each other. This is a highly creative, flagrantly sexual time which is expressed through the many fertility symbols that characterize this festival, such as bonfires — which were traditionally lit to ensure fertility to the household and farmyard — dancing around the maypole and jumping over a fire contained within a cauldron.

Ritual

New unions are created during this festival, which may prove disruptive to our old life. As we commit in ritual to a certain path, the energies around us are realigned so that we are able to progress. Important magical work can be achieved at Beltane because the veil between the worlds is again thin. As at Samhain, contact can be made with the dead, but in Wiccan beliefs this is not the same as summoning the spirits to do your bidding. The main purpose of contact with a departed friend or relative is to give comfort or receive wisdom.

Litha (Midsummer Solstice)

Litha represents the time of fulfillment. The goddess is growing in her joy, filled with love and the expectation of a new child. The sun is at the highest point in the heavens. However, there is also change because once he has reached his full height, the god begins to become introspective and to accept that his path leads gradually to darkness and death. His strength will wane, echoed in the season as the days become shorter.

Ritual

Rituals at Litha can be potent with the veils between the worlds being at their thinnest. If you decide to celebrate this festival with any working of energies, particularly sexual energy, it would be a very good idea to do a grounding visualization, such as imagining your body as a tree, its trunk your spine and its roots your energy linking into the ground. Take stock and notice the fulfillment of some of your achievements and feel how your life is corresponding with the Wheel of the Year.

Opposite: Dancing around a maypole, *as depicted here by* Pieter Brueghel the Younger (c.1564 – 1638), *is a tradition at* Beltane.

Right: Litha *falls at midsummer, a time when fulfillment reaches its peak before the next cycle.*

Lammas

The festival of Lammas represents a time of sacrifice when the god has used the last of his energy to bring forth a bountiful harvest. The goddess nurtures the god's energy and ensures that a harvest of golden fruits, vegetables and grains emerges from the earth. However, a price has been paid for the bounty.

Ritual

Lammas rituals observe the god's death and the earth's harvest. It is a time for you to acknowledge the sacrifices that you have made during the year to provide your own harvest, whether it be through monetary gains, love or career advancements. It is a time to understand that how you have worked and what you have sacrificed will reflect in how bountiful your harvest will be at this time. If your harvest is meager, learn from your mistakes and try again next year. Rituals held during this time can be devised for the purpose of helping you rededicate your spiritual purpose.

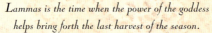

Lammas is the time when the power of the goddess
helps bring forth the last harvest of the season.

With winter approaching, a balance between darkness and light is kept during Mabon.

Mabon (Autumn Equinox)

Mabon is a time of primary harvest and for sorting what we will need for winter. It is a time of balance between light and dark, but the cycle looks toward the god's retreat into the underworld. As the goddess sees the harvest being drawn in, rituals can involve charging the seed for next year's harvest. All the sabbats have strong emphasis on balance — between light and dark, the feminine and the masculine, and between life and death.

Ritual

Rituals held during this time focus on again giving thanks to the Lord and the Lady for whatever was "harvested" and ritual preparations are made for the quiet time of winter ahead. Winter is a fallow time, and Mabon rituals may help focus your mind on what study and resolutions you may need to follow in this quiet time. It is a time to ask for guidance in using the time during winter wisely so that your energy reserves build to a peak that will power you through to the Midsummer Solstice. You may ask for guidance in the development of your inner self.

CHART OF SEASONAL CORRESPONDENCES

Samhain

Other names – Halloween, All Saints Day

Meaning – The peace of the womb before birth and the peace of the world beyond death

Rituals – Honoring the dead

Herbs/flowers/plants – Sage, cornstalks

Stones – Ruby

Colors – Black, red

Elements – Fire

Planets – Mars

Zodiac – Scorpio

Imbolc

Other names – Candlemas, Feast of St. Brigid, Groundhog day

Meaning – End of darkness and reaffirmation of growth

Rituals – Purification

Herbs/flowers/plants – Lavender

Stones – Turquoise

Colors – White

Elements – Water

Planets – Uranus

Zodiac – Aquarius

Yule

Other names – Midwinter solstice, Christmas

Meaning – Rebirth of the Sun after the longest night

Rituals – Celebration of birth and growth

Herbs/flowers/plants – Chamomile, frankincense, holly, mistletoe, pine, evergreen

Stones – Onyx, jet, obsidian

Colors – Red, Orange

Elements – Earth

Planets – Saturn

Zodiac – Capricorn

Ostara

Other names – Spring equinox, Easter

Meaning – Birth, growth and new fertility

Rituals – Planting flowers and trees

Herbs/flowers/plants – Tansy, honeysuckle and bulb flowers such as daffodils

Stones – Ruby

Colors – Green, yellow

Elements – Fire

Planets – Mars

Zodiac – Aries

Beltane

Other names — May Day, Feast of the Cross
Meaning — Realization of fertility
Rituals — Honoring the earth
Herbs/flowers/plants — Frankincense, marigold, rose
Stones — Emerald, jade
Colors — Orange
Elements — Earth
Planets — Venus
Zodiac — Taurus

Lammas

Other names — Lughnasad, feast day for the Virgin Mary
Meaning — Increasing plenty and decreasing light
Rituals — Rededication
Herbs/flowers/plants — Frankincense, sunflower
Stones — Topaz
Colors — Golden yellow
Elements — Fire
Planet — Sun
Zodiac — Leo

Litha

Other names — Midsummer solstice
Meaning — Maturity and consummation
Rituals — Great Rite, divination
Herbs/flowers/plants — Chamomile, fennel, St. John's Wort, rose
Stones — Moonstone, quartz crystal, pearl
Colors — Green, orange
Elements — Water
Planet — Moon
Zodiac — Cancer

Mabon

Other names — Autumn equinox
Meaning — Completed harvest and preparation for the quiet time
Rituals — Guidance for resolutions and study
Herbs/flowers/plants — Myrrh, sage, marigold, passion flower, white rose
Stones — Emerald, jade
Colors — Purple
Elements — Air
Planet — Venus
Zodiac — Libra

DAILY OBSERVANCES

Keeping in Tune with Your Magical Intention

There are a number of important daily exercises that is recommended for people wishing to practice white magic. Two exercises in particular should be mastered – grounding (*see* page 40) and centering (*see* next page).

The Importance of Grounding

We have already outlined one version of grounding which helps us feel linked to the vital energy of the earth – visualizing yourself as a tree with roots digging deep down into the soil. This is only one of many such techniques. It is very important to ground yourself after a ritual and, if you find this difficult, to ground everyday until it becomes second nature. The danger of failing to ground is a sense of being unsettled and feeling aimless and disoriented. It is an unpleasant aftermath to the raising of strong energy in a Circle. The energy raised must go somewhere. Most of it goes toward your Circle work but the remainder can make it difficult to re-enter the real world. Try to incorporate a grounding exercise each day for a year and a day. This commitment will soon repay the effort as you will experience a sense of well-being and stability increasing in your life.

Another technique for grounding is a simple yet powerful visualization of a cord extending through your spine and into the center of the earth. Imagine the central vertical axis of your body aligning with that cord. This visualization may be performed in either a seated or standing position, depending on how much physical exertion you wish to include.

Centering Yourself

As you are standing with your feet and knees together, attempt to feel the muscles in the front of your legs pushing back against those in the back of your legs. Feel the interplay of the muscles. Once you have balanced the sensation in the front and back of your legs, try it from the sides, the right and left side of your leg muscles pushing inward. Allow this feeling to travel up the trunk of your body.

What you should be feeling, if you haven't fallen over, is your body working to balance itself. By learning to pull in your body into its center you are helping the mind accomplish the same result so that it can collect its straying energies and concentrate them into your core. You could also imagine that you are a tree being buffeted by the winds of the four elements — air, fire, water and earth. By combining the mind's effort with the body's, you will start to feel integrated and balanced within your body and your soul. You energy will increase dramatically.

Keeping a Diary

As a summary, other daily observances that we have suggested throughout the book include keeping a diary of your everyday life. Every sabbat bring your diary into Circle and before closing, take a moment to review the last six weeks of your life and see if events follow at all the season's essence. It is a good idea to keep a journal of your spiritual experiences and insights, felt both inside and outside Circle. The main aim of all these practices is to integrate the everyday world with your spiritual one, allowing you to make your magic work successfully outside your mind and make a real difference in the world.

BREATHING EXERCISES

The Key to the Control of Your Conscious Mind

Breath control is one of the key techniques that help you alter your state of consciousness by enabling you to focus on the energy flowing through your body. Many spiritual disciplines, particularly in the East, focus on the importance of breathing deeply and slowly. Controlled breathing affects your heart rate and allows you to concentrate on your body and its link with the earth. If you have difficulty meditating because you find yourself easily distracted, you will be amazed how effortlessly you will be able to overcome these distractions by focusing solely on your breath. It is believed that certain breathing techniques will energize your body with the universal life force.

Basic Breathing Technique for Meditation

A good introduction to meditation can be through the technique of rhythmic breathing, where breathing is held to a regular pattern of inhalation, holding, exhalation and again holding. This rhythm is maintained by counting, such as breathe in for a count of eight, hold for four, breathe out for eight and hold for four. This is the simplest technique for breath control. It is useful also for relaxation purposes and for relieving panic attacks.

When practicing this technique, do not worry if thoughts stray into your consciousness. Acknowledge them, then allow them to float away. Imagine unhooking yourself from them. When you wish to finish your session, wriggle your toes and stretch your limbs to signal your return to external consciousness.

Pore Breathing and Transforming the Breath into Energy

There are a series of exercises that focus on breathing through the pores of your entire body. These exercises, for obvious reasons, are best practiced skyclad (naked) or in a minimum of light, loose-fitting clothing. Imagine that with each breath you take, your body is filling with healing energy through the pores of the skin and that with each exhalation, your body is expelling unwanted energy through its pores.

Once you have mastered this stage of the technique, try focusing on different parts of the body. Imagine your breath traveling to your hand or the chakra centers that run through the trunk of your body or to an area in your body that is feeling constricted or ill at ease. Sometimes, certain thoughts that stray into your mind as you focus on an unhappy part of your body are insights into why you are experiencing discomfort in that area. Take heed of those thoughts and allow your breath to help clear the problem or constriction.

The next stage to conquer is to transform the inhalation into a form of energy before releasing it. This can be most effective when working spells for protection and healing. You may wish to cast a protective spell. Imagine that your indrawn breath is a gentle blue shade. The blue signifies harmonization with your intention, in this case, the protection of your friend or relative. Imagine this blue breath mingling with your intention and then, with the next exhalation, your breath and your intention are a particular form of energy.

For a healing spell, you may focus your breath into your hands, and as you inhale, imagine your breath turning into an energy suitable for the healing. As you exhale, feel the breath and its heat coming through your hands as you place your hand over the affected area. Allow the magic to do its work.

WITCHCRAFT ETHICS AND ADVICE

Starting Out

If you find that you enjoy working with the energy of the earth and your soul yearns for deeper connections with other people who are of a similar mind, there are a few points to keep in mind when looking for teachers and working partners in magic.

From this book and through our suggested reading list you will get a clear picture of the types of magic you will enjoy and those you could live without. Use you inner wisdom to assess which path of magic you should walk down first. The beauty of magic is that there are so many paths you can explore, you could even devote a lifetime of study to magic and not be bored. As so often happens, once you have committed yourself to the study of the right strand of magic for you, the information you need to set you on your path will materialize.

Concerning Teachers and Groups

When choosing a teacher, beware of people who are quick to "initiate" you into his or her path of magic or who seek to control your experiences in magic. Evaluate how comfortable you feel around the people you seek as teachers or as working partners. Use your intuition. If you don't feel comfortable or are unsure, it is best not to share your sacred space or do workings with these people until you are truly happy with the energy that you feel about a particular person or group. As in life — so in magic. Search for people who are sincere, caring and reliable. Although it might not have the glamor of certain more flamboyant witches and wizards, dependability in a working partner, teacher or group will be of more benefit to your development in the long run.

Working as a Solitary

Working magic as a solitary or "hedge witch" can be a safe way of entering a life of magic. It is not necessary to rigidly follow the path of Wicca, the kabbala or other traditions or systems. A witch or wizard is free to pick and choose aspects of occult techniques and evolve his or her own personal magic.

It is always wise to work on balancing your physical, emotional and intellectual life as you develop your skills in magic. Working as a solitary allows you to work at your own pace and avoid the checks, strains and compromises of coven life. As a witch or wizard you will find that your work stems from finding the balance of the elements and what they symbolize in yourself, your lifestyle and your magic. It is believed by many pagans that to balance air (the intellect), fire (the will), water (the emotions) and earth (the body) is to manifest your true power in life. Being a solitary witch can sometimes be a lonely existence. An agreeable way of attuning to what is happening in occult circles is to visit some of the open festivals sometimes celebrated by pagans and non-pagans alike and various New Age symposiums that disseminate information on newly researched or devised techniques that could be of interest to you in your workings.

Working within a Coven

A modern coven can range in membership from three people to the traditional thirteen members. The ideal coven is one in which you are able to develop individually along your chosen path but share your knowledge with the rest of the group in an atmosphere of "Perfect Love and Perfect Trust".

Above: A coven provides its members a place to perform important rituals, including handfasting, a Wiccan form of marriage.

Opposite: Your true path will provide a deeper connection with the energy of the earth.

There are many advantages in forming your own coven or seeking admittance into an already established one. A coven can help keep people a little more grounded in reality and can provide assistance should any working go astray. As in many creative teams, working magic as a group often works as synergy, where the energy raised by the group as a whole is greater than the sum of energy that would be raised by each individual alone.

Care must be taken when working in covens because the intimacy experienced by coven members in circles can produce severe emotional tensions unless it is monitored carefully. Apart from occasionally needing to alter your working style to harmonize with the other members of your coven, the feeling of having a family that understands you can be very powerful.

Even if you find the perfect coven, it is still very important to keep true to yourself. No matter what, do not allow any individual, group or institution to override your gut feelings about a particular practice. Always keep true to your own path, strengthening your will, for this is the most powerful magic.

GLOSSARY OF SYMBOLS

✝ **Ankh**: an Egyptian hieroglyphic symbolizing immortality.

Astrological: astrological symbols were developed over the centuries and were strongly influenced by the symbols found in Cornelius Agrippa's book *De Occulta Philosophia* (1513):

	Modern	Agrippa
Aries	♈	V
Taurus	♉	♉
Gemini	♊	♊
Cancer	♋	⊷
Leo	♌	♌
Virgo	♍	♍
Libra	♎	♎
Scorpio	♏	♏
Sagittarius	♐	↑
Capricorn	♑	♑
Aquarius	♒	♒
Pisces	♓	♓

○ **Circle**: symbolizes spirit.

✝ **Cross (Christian)**: symbolizing the immortality of Jesus Christ and all those who follow him.

✚ **Cross (equal-armed)**: symbolizes matter.

Cross (inverted): symbolizes Satanism.

Elemental: the four elemental signs use the triangle as the basic form:

△ **Fire**: the upright triangle indicates the upward motion of the flames.

▽ **Water**: the upturned triangle indicates the motion of rivers running deep into the earth.

△ **Air**: the upright triangle with a line through it indicates that air is perceived to harmonize with fire.

▽ **Earth**: the upturned triangle with a line through it indicates that earth harmonizes with water.

Eye: symbolizes the spirit within and can be used as a protection against evil. Often inscribed on amulets and on the prow of boats. The Eye of Horus is particularly popular Egyptian symbol of the all-seeing power of the higher being.

 Hexagram (Six-pointed star): the Star of David is a symbol of the Jewish faith. In occult terms, the symbol is also known as the Seal of Solomon, symbolizing the harmonization of the four symbols of the elements. It is thought to "unveil all of nature's powers". Under Hermetic principles, the six-pointed star symbolizes the concept of "as above, so below". The star was also used as a symbol of the Hermetic Order of the Golden Dawn.

 Hexagram (Unicursal): a symbol devised by Aleister Crowley and used as a symbol of his Order of the Silver Star.

 Labrys: symbolizes the strength of matriarchy. This symbol is sometimes used by Dianic covens and initiates.

 Pentacle (upright): the five-pointed star represents the four elements and the spirit, and is a popular symbol for witchcraft.

 Pentacle (upside down): symbolizes Satanism.

PLANTEARY SYMBOLS:

⊙ **Sun**

☽ **Moon**

⊕ **Earth**

☿ **Mercury**

♀ **Venus**

♂ **Mars**

♃ **Jupiter**

♄ **Saturn**

♅ **Uranus**

♆ **Neptune**

♇ **Pluto**

Seasonal Symbols:

♏ **Autumn**

♉ **Spring**

♋ **Summer**

♒ **Winter**

◊ **Vesica Piscis**: symbolizes resurrection in Christian terminology and is thought to be an Egyptian hieroglyphic symbolizing a doorway or the gate of birth.

✳ **Wheel of the Year**: the eight spokes within a circle symbolizes the cyclic nature of each of the eight sabbats.

GLOSSARY OF TERMS

Alexandrian: Wiccans initiated by Alex and Maxine Sanders or stemming from those who have been initiated by the Sanders.

Amulet: an object with magical properties of protection.

Aradia: Wiccan name for the goddess, derived from C.G. Leland's manuscript *Aradia: the Gospel of the Witches*.

Astral projection: a technique to move the conscious to the astral plane while leaving the body behind.

Athame: a black-handled knife used for casting a circle around your sacred space. Witches and wizards usually have their own personal athame. It is bad manners to touch another's athame without permission. Athames are an important elemental tool symbolizing air.

Beltane: one of the four Greater Sabbats. Known as May Eve in the northern hemisphere.

Blessed Be: traditional greeting and blessing used by witches and wizards.

Book of Shadows: a personal journal compiled by the witch or wizard, containing spells, rituals and observations.

Cernunnos: name of the Celtic horned god.

Chakra: a line of energy running through a number of energy centers of the body. Normally there are seven chakra centers, starting from the base of the spine and ending at the top of the head.

Charge of the God: the words spoken by the god through the individual who performs the Drawing down the Sun ritual.

Charge of the Goddess: the words spoken by the goddess through the individual who performs the Drawing down the Moon ritual.

Chalice: or cup, one of the elemental tools symbolizing water.

Charm: a magical word or words that can be used as a protection.

Circle: a sacred space, usually thought of as a sphere of energy created when the Circle is cast.

Cone of power: raising the energy within the Circle to a peak that can then be directed to the purpose in mind.

Coven: a group of witches, ranging in number from three to thirteen, who meet regularly to perform and discuss magic.

Craft, The: a popular name for witchcraft.

Divination: techniques used to divine the future or a person's path. Such techniques include scrying, tarot cards, reading tea leaves and palmistry.

Drawing down the Moon: a ritual to bring down or channel the higher female energy into the individual.

Drawing down the Sun: a ritual to bring down or channel the higher male energy into the individual.

Esbat: a ritual or meeting conducted during full moon.

Gardnerians: Wiccans initiated by Gerald Gardner or stemming from those initiated by Gardner.

Golden Dawn: an occult order founded in the late-nineteenth century known as the Hermetic Order of the Golden Dawn.

Grimoire: a book that is a compilation of a number of spells, techniques and mysteries that have been used over a period of time.

Grounding: a term referring to connecting the body's energy with that of the earth.

Herne: otherwise known as Herne the Hunter, a popular British god.

High Priest: in a group working, the male leader.

High Priestess: in a group working, the female leader.

Imbolc: one of the four **Greater Sabbats**, known as **Candlemas** in the northern hemisphere.

Invoke: to summon a spirit or energy form into oneself.

Kabbala: a **Jewish** mystical tradition that structures the levels of existence along the form of a tree.

Lammas: one of the four **Greater Sabbats**. **Known** as Lughnasadh in the northern hemisphere.

Litha: midsummer solstice.

Mabon: autumn equinox.

Necromancy: summoning the spirits of the dead to do the summoner's bidding.

Ostara: spring equinox.

Pagan: a general term used for people who are not **Christians**.

Pentacle: a five-pointed star made of metal or other material that is the symbol of the four elements and the spirit and can be worn as a protection. The pentacle is also an important elemental tool symbolizing earth. If it is upright, with the point uppermost, the pentacle is a symbol of **Wicca**. If it is upside down, with the point at the bottom, the pentacle is a symbol of **Satanism**.

Pentagram: a five-pointed figure that is used as a blessing by witches and wizards.

Power animal: an animal or thought form of an animal with specific psychic attributes or protective qualities.

Sabbat: the eight seasonal festivals during a **Wiccan** year.

Samhain: one of the four **Greater Sabbats**, known as Halloween in the northern hemisphere.

Scrying: a form of divination using reflective surfaces, such as a crystal ball.

Sephiroth: the ten levels of energies that form the Tree of Life in the **Kabbala**.

Shapeshifter: someone who is able to change shape at will. This can refer to changing one's actual shape or the way that people perceive one.

Sigil: a special sign that incorporates a form of magical energy.

Skyclad: means naked. The term is derived from the translation of an Indian term meaning "clad by the sky" which was first used in reference to the practice of witchcraft by Gerald Gardner.

So Mote It Be: a Wiccan equivalent of the Christian "Amen".

Talisman: an object charged with a specific magical purpose.

Triple goddess: refers to the three faces of the goddess, the Maid (virgin), the Mother and the Crone.

Wand: an important elemental tool symbolizing fire.

Wicca: Old English name for the practice of witchcraft.

Wiccan: an individual, male or female, who practices witchcraft.

Witch: traditionally a female witch. However, in modern times refers to both male and female witches.

Wizard: traditionally a male witch. However, in modern times a male also carries the title of witch.

Working: a Wiccan synonym for a magical ritual.

Yule: midwinter solstice.

READING LIST

M. Adler, *Drawing Down the Moon* (Boston, Beacon Press, 1981)

D. Ashcroft-Nowicki, *Daughters of Eve: The Magical Mysteries of Womanhood.* (London, Aquarian, 1993)

R. Buckland, *Buckland's Complete Book of Witchcraft* (St Paul, Llewellyn Publications, 1987)

P. Beyerl, *The Master Book of Herbalism* (Washington, Phoenix Publishing Co, 1984)

A. Crowley, *777 Revised* (New York, Weiser, 1970)

V. Crowley, *Wicca: The Old Religion in the New Age* (London, Aquarian Press, 1989)

S. Cunningham,
Wicca: A Guide for the Solitary Practitioner (St Paul, Llewellyn, 1988)
The Complete Book of Incense, Oils and Brews (St Paul, Llewellyn, 1990)
Cunningham's Encyclopedia of Magical Herbs (St Paul, Llewellyn, 1990)
Earth, Air, Fire and Water (St Paul, Llewellyn, 1992)
Magical Herbalism (St Paul, Llewellyn, 1989)
The Magic in Food: Legends, Lore & Spellwork (St Paul, Llewellyn, 1991)

N. Drury, *The Occult Experience* (London, Robert Hale, 1987)
Inner Visions: Explorations in Magical Consciousness (London, Routledge & Kegan Paul, 1979)

D. Fortune, *The Mystical Qabalah* (New York, Ibis Books, 1981 reprint)

D. Fortune, novels
The Demon Lover (London, Wyndham Publications, 1976 reprint)
Moon Magic (London, Wyndham Publications, 1976 reprint)
The Goat-Foot God (London, Wyndham Publications, 1976 reprint)
The Winged Bull (London, Wyndham Publications, 1976 reprint)
The Sea Priestess (London, Wyndham Publications, 1976 reprint)

G. B. Gardner, *Meaning of Witchcraft* (New York, Magickal Childe, Inc, 1982 reprint)

S. Farrar, novels
The Twelve Maidens: A Novel of Witchcraft (London, Arrow Books, 1976)
The Sword of Orley (London, Arrow Books, 1978)
Omega (New York, Times Books, 1980)

J. & S. Farrar, *Eight Sabbats for Witches and rites for Birth, Marriage and Death* (London, Robert Hale, 1981)
Spells and How They Work (London, Robert Hale, 1990)
The Life and Times of a Modern Witch (London, Judy Piatkus (Publishers) Limited, 1987)
The Witches' God: Lord of the Dance (London, Robert Hale, 1989)
The Witches' Goddess: The Feminine Principle of Divinity (London, Robert Hale, 1987)
The Witches' Way: Principles, Rituals and Beliefs of Modern Witchcraft (London, Robert Hale, 1984)
What Witches Do: The Modern Coven Revealed (Washington, Phoenix Publishing Co, 1983)

R. Guiley, *The Encyclopedia of Witches and Witchcraft* (New York, Facts on File, 1989)

F. Horne, *Witch: A Personal Journey* (Sydney, Randon House, 1998)

M. Jordan, *Witches: An Encyclopedia of Paganism and Magic* (London, Kyle Cathie, 1996)

M. Medici, *Good Magic* (London, Macmillan, 1988)

T. Moorey, *Witchcraft: a beginner's guide* (London, Hodder & Stoughton, 1996)

Paganism: a beginner's guide (London, Hodder & Stoughton, 1996)

D. and J. Parker, *The Power of Magic: Secrets and Mysteries Ancient and Modern* (London, Mitchell Beazley, 1992)

I. Shah, *The Secret Lore of Magic* (London, Rider, 1990)

"Starhawk", *The Spiral Dance: A Rebirth of the Ancient Religion of the Great Goddess* (San Francisco, Harper & Row, 1979)

D. Stein, *The Women's Book of Healing* (St Paul, Llewellyn, 1989)

D. Valiente, *Natural Magic* (London, Robert Hale, 1985 reprint)
An ABC of Witchcraft Past and Present (London, Robert Hale, 1984 reprint)
Witchcraft for Tomorrow (London, Robert Hale, 1978)

L. Warren-Clarke, *The Way of the Goddess: A Manual for Wiccan Initiation* (Dorset, Prism Unity, 1987)

C. Wilson, *Aleister Crowley: The Nature of the Beast* (London, The Aquarian Press, 1987)

PICTURE CREDITS

The authors are particularly grateful to Nevill Drury for his generous assistance and support. The publishers would like to thank the following organisations for the provision of the pictures used in this publication. Full effort has been made to locate all the copyright owners of the images and we apologize for any omissions or errors.

The Bridgeman Art Library, London/New York

cover & page 10: A Sorceress, probably Circe, with a cup of poison for Odysseus and his companions, 1493 (woodcut) by German School (fifteenth century), from the Nuremberg Chronicle by Hartmann Schedel (1440–1514) – Stapleton Collection, UK
page 2: The Alchemist from a book on the Philosopher's Stone, German, 1582 Tractatus Alchymicae Germanick Splendor Solis, 1589 – British Library, London
page 9: The Triumph of St Augustine, 1664, by Coello – Prado, Madrid, Spain
page 11: Medea by Anselm Feuerbach (1829–80) – Kunsthistorisches Museum, Vienna, Austria
page 13: The Beguiling of Merlin from Idylls of the King by Alfred Tennyson (1809–92), 1870–74, painted by Sir Edward Burne-Jones (1833–98) – Lady Lever Art Gallery, Port Sunlight, Merseyside, UK/London Board of Trustees: National Museums & Galleries on Merseyside
page 15: White Horse Hill, Uffington, 1992 (w/c), by Evangeline Dickson (living artist) – private collection
page 17: The Flyer, a Native American Shaman, c.1570 (w/c), by John White (fl.c.1570–93) – British Museum, London
page 20: The Voodoo Divinities, Damballah, la Flambeau and Jean Danton by Andre Pierre (1914–79) – private collection
page 29: Portrait of the Physician Paracelsus (1493–1541) by Quentin Massys (c.1466–1530) – Louvre, Paris, France/Giraudon
page 33: Illustration from Theosophica Practica showing the seven Chakras, nineteenth century – private collection
page 47: Glastonbury Tor (w/c on paper) by Osmund Caine – private collection
page 77: Votive statuette of Isis suckling the child Horus, Late Period Egyptian c.664–334 BC (bronze), found at Saqqarah together with original wooden throne and base – Ashmolean Museum, Oxford, UK
page 78: Diana the Huntress by Gaston Casimir Saintpierre (1833–1916) – private collection
page 90: Peony: Paeonia officinalis, c.1568, by J.le Moyne de Morgue (c.1530–88) – Victoria and Albert Museum, London
page 95: Astrological Map from the Sea Atlas by Johannes Van Keulen, c.1800 – Royal Geographical Society, London, UK

page 97: *Pan and Psyche* by Sir Edward Burne-Jones (1833–98) – Agnew & Sons, London

page 98: *Odin, ancestor of Father Christmas*, anonymous illustration – private collection

page 99: *Statue of the Cult of Osiris* – Louvre, Paris

page 101: *The Sun Rises While the Moon Sleeps*, 1990, by Peter Davidson (living artist) – private collection

page 103: *Druids Sacrificing to the Sun in their Temple called Stonehenge* from a plan of Stonehenge by Dr Stukeley in the Ashmolean Museum, by Nathaniel Whittock (1791–1860) – Stapleton Collection, UK

page 105: *Masonic Regalia*, from the Order of Turin – private collection

page 121: *Spring Tide near Honfleur*, c.1861, by Paul Huet (1803–69) – Louvre, Paris

page 123: *Night* by Giuseppe Bonito (1707–89) – private collection

page 128: *Fairy Wood* by John Hassell (1767–1825) – Lincolnshire Country Council, Usher Gallery, Lincoln, UK

page 130: *A Village Kermesse and Peasants Dancing Around a Maypole* by Pieter the Younger Brueghel (c.1564–1638) – Christie's Images

page 131: "*Summer*" from *The Seasons* commissioned for the 1920 *Pears Annual* by Charles Robinson (1870–1937)

Cinetel Productions/Collection of Nevill Drury

page 37; page 38; page 53; page 59; page 127; page 142

The Granger Collection, New York

page 25: Illustration of Salem "witch" trials by Howard Pyle

Images Colour Library, London: Charles Walker Collection

page 23: *Malleus Maleficarum*, title page of the Lugduni (Lyons) edition, 1669

International Photo Library

page 5; page 45; page 54; page 64, page 68: pages 72–3; page 81; page 114; page 126, page 132, page 143

Lansdowne Publishing Pty Ltd

page 50; page: 67; page 88; page 89; page 91; and all symbols and line drawings produced by the designer for this publication

Mary Evans Picture Library

page 42: 17th century woodcut of dowser

Photo Library

page 19; page 34; page 41; page 43; page 56–7; page 70 (poppet); page 93; page 111; page 112; page 113; page 119; page 129, page 133

INDEX

MetroBooks

An Imprint of Friedman/Fairfax Publishers

This edition published by MetroBooks by arrangement with
Lansdowne Publishing

ISBN 1-5866-3755-X
1 3 5 7 9 10 8 6 4 2

For bulk purchases and special sales, please contact:
Friedman/Fairfax Publishers
Attention: Sales Department
230 Fifth Avenue, Suite 700
New York, NY 10001
212/685-6610 FAX 212/685-3916

Visit our website:
www.metrobooks.com

Copyright design and text © 1998 Lansdowne Publishing Pty Ltd
Copyright pictures © as per Picture Credits list

Publisher: Deborah Nixon
Production Manager: Kristy Nelson
Editor: Cynthia Blanche
Designer: Robyn Latimer
Project co-ordinator/picture research: Joanne Holliman

Set in Nicolas Cochin on QuarkXpress
Printed in Hong Kong by South China Printing